Engaging Students in Disciplinary Literacy, K–6

Reading, Writing, and Teaching Tools for the Classroom

CYNTHIA H. BROCK, VIRGINIA J. GOATLEY, TAFFY E. RAPHAEL,
ELISABETH TROST-SHAHATA, AND CATHERINE M. WEBER

All About Words

Increasing Vocabulary in the Common Core Classroom, PreK–2

SUSAN B. NEUMAN AND TANYA WRIGHT

Engaging Students in Disciplinary Literacy, K–6

READING, WRITING, AND TEACHING TOOLS FOR THE CLASSROOM

Cynthia H. Brock
Virginia J. Goatley
Taffy E. Raphael
Elisabeth Trost-Shahata
Catherine M. Weber

FOREWORD BY
Annemarie Sullivan Palincsar

TEACHERS COLLEGE PRESS
TEACHERS COLLEGE | COLUMBIA UNIVERSITY
NEW YORK AND LONDON

Published by Teachers College Press, 1234 Amsterdam Avenue, New York, NY 10027

Figure 4.2 is reprinted from *Two in the Wilderness*, by Sandra Weber (2005), Calkin Creek Books, Honesdale, PA. Copyright by Boyds Mills Press. Used by permission.

The photographs inside this book were taken by Cynthia H. Brock. Used by permission.

Library of Congress Cataloging-in-Publication Data

Brock, Cynthia H.
    Engaging students in disciplinary literacy, K–6 : reading, writing, and teaching tools for the classroom / Cynthia H. Brock, Virginia J. Goatley, Taffy E. Raphael, Elisabeth Trost-Shahata, Catherine M. Weber ; foreword by Annemarie Sullivan Palincsar.
        pages cm. — (Common core state standards in literacy series)
    Includes bibliographical references and index.
    ISBN 978-0-8077-5527-3 (pbk. : alk. paper)
    ISBN 978-0-8077-7283-6 (ebook)
    1. Content area reading—Study and teaching (Elementary)—United States.
    2. Language arts (Elementary)—United States. I. Goatley, Virginia J.
    II. Raphael, Taffy. III. Trost-Shahata, Elisabeth. IV. Weber, Catherine M. V. Title.
    LB1050.455.B75 2014
    372.6—dc23   2014007323

ISBN 978-0-8077-5527-3 (paperback)
ISBN 978-0-8077-7283-6 (ebook)

Printed on acid-free paper
Manufactured in the United States of America

This book is dedicated to the many collaborative colleagues, reflective teachers, and thoughtful learners we have encountered in U.S. classrooms and abroad.

Contents

Foreword

If you love to travel, you probably have your favorite line of guidebooks. Great travel guides are the result of: careful research, the right blending of general and specific information, an enthusiastic spirit that energizes the traveler, and imagination that fuels the thinking and planning of the user. Why is this germane to *Engaging Students in Disciplinary Literacy*? I believe that what Cynthia Brock, Virginia Goatley, Taffy Raphael, Elisabeth Trost-Shahata, and Catherine M. Weber have created is just that—a terrific travel guide for the educator who is venturing into the new frontier that is being forged by the Common Core State Standards (CCSS). I will say a bit about each of the features that I associate with a top-rate travel guide and how they are reflected in this volume.

With respect to research, the authors have clearly done their homework. They draw upon cutting-edge theoretical and empirical work that has been conducted by scholars in the field of language literacy—which these authors represent—as well as by scholars who have studied domain-specific teaching and learning in the social studies, natural sciences, and mathematics. This means that the reader is equipped with current research on text comprehension and research that has been conducted to explore the disciplinary-specific ways in which reading, writing, and oral language are used to inform, argue, and persuade. This research is complemented by the authors' own inquiry in classrooms in grades 2, 4, and 6. Presented with instructional vignettes, samples of classroom conversation, illustrations of assessments and curriculum plans, the classroom-based research that is presented throughout the volume inspires confidence and helps to map the terrain in supportive and generative ways.

The authors have achieved a fine balance in the grain size of the information they present. There are five guiding design principles, which are written with sufficient breadth and comprehensiveness that they apply across grade levels and content areas. However, the principles do not stand alone in this volume. Instead, they are richly illustrated with concrete steps that serve to guide instructional decisionmaking. Taken together, the principles and specific practices presented in this volume demystify a number of the most daunting aspects of the CCSS, for example, what engagement in *close reading* looks like; how to evaluate *text complexity*; how to teach *disciplinary literacy* even with young elementary students; how to enact ambitious instruction that is also motivating to diverse classrooms of learners; and how to teach reading, writing, and oral language as tools to acquire knowledge about the world and oneself.

The energizing dimension of this guide is perhaps best captured by a quotation from the first chapter:

> What a joy to be mandated to teach to high levels of thinking, prepare our students for a lifetime of success and personal satisfaction, engage in interesting work to learn about the physical and social world, and engage with one another in debate, argumentation, and persuasion using what was learned through their exploration of new content.

Were this simply lofty rhetoric, the words might ring hollow. However, the authors—particularly through vignettes of classroom instruction—convey the satisfaction and interestingness that can be achieved when students are, for example, supported to confront the limitations of presentism as historians must to provide useful accounts of historical figures or to engage in critical civic inquiry about how tax dollars are spent in a community.

Finally, I have argued that a good travel guide fuels the user's imagination in the sense that armed with sufficient knowledge of the culture, customs, and geography, the traveler might be more inclined to go "off the beaten path" and create his or her own adventure. The resources that are provided in this volume are imaginative resources that can, in fact, transform teaching. These resources are in the form of helpful literature reviews, ideas for essential questions to drive students' inquiry, illustrations of how oral and written language can be taught in the service of advancing knowledge building with text, and specific discourse moves that educators use to mediate students' sense-making. I believe that this is the most important contribution of this volume: If teachers are supported—and support one another—to enact the principles and practices that are presented in this volume, this will be the most important legacy of the CCSS movement, regardless of the vagaries of the political process associated with the movement. So, intrepid traveler, immerse yourself in this trusty guide, venture forth, and join fellow educators in forging a new frontier.

Annemarie Sullivan Palincsar

Preface

Two spheres of influence have coalesced to bring about the work we share in this book. First, the rollout of the Common Core State Standards (CCSS) has reinforced the importance of disciplinary instruction at all educational levels, including the elementary grades. This represents a significant shift from the decade-long focus on foundational skills at the elementary level under No Child Left Behind. Second, adolescent literacy scholars (e.g., Draper, 2008, Moje, 2007; Shanahan & Shanahan, 2008) have called into question the practice of using generic literacy skills in the disciplines at the middle and high school levels. Instead, they propose a framework for instruction—called disciplinary literacy—that focuses on using reading, writing, and talk as tools for learning in unique and discipline-specific ways. Uniting these major spheres of influence in this book, we explore the process and outcome of working together with content specialists, literacy scholars, classroom teachers, and students to develop, teach, and reflect on disciplinary literacy instruction in the elementary grades. A unique contribution of this book is the focus on disciplinary literacy teaching and learning at the elementary level.

This book addresses elementary teachers' needs, introducing key concepts from current trends in literacy education, from high-level standards to the use of 21st-century literacies as tools to explore disciplinary content. The book highlights the implementation of three disciplinary literacy units of instruction—a science unit in a 2nd-grade classroom, a social studies (history) unit in a 4th-grade classroom, and a mathematics unit in a 6th-grade classroom. Each unit revolves around a central inquiry question. The teachers featured in the book successfully implement instruction in the elementary grades to promote high-level thinking and engagement with disciplinary content. Within each chapter, we address implications of using Common Core for curriculum development and instruction, situated in research-based best practices.

The first section of the book includes two chapters that provide an overview of the conceptual content for the rest of the book. In Chapter 1, the introduction, we situate our framework in the current educational context, introduce disciplinary literacy, and discuss its relationship to the CCSS. We describe reading, writing, and talking as conceptual tools to foster disciplinary literacy learning. We address both opportunities and cautions for the use of the CCSS related to the implementation of curriculum and instruction. We also introduce five research-based principles of effective instruction that we weave throughout the remaining chapters in the book. Chapter 2 provides an in-depth examination of disciplinary literacy and why it is important for teaching in elementary classrooms. We briefly introduce readers to the three classrooms (lower, middle, and upper elementary) featured in this book and the disciplinary literacy units we enacted in each class.

Chapters 3, 4, and 5 comprise the second section of the book, drawing on the three classrooms introduced in Chapter 2. These three chapters—the heart of the book—provide vivid windows into classroom teaching and learning showing how reading (Chapter 3), writing (Chapter 4), and talk (Chapter 5) serve as tools to foster disciplinary learning across the elementary grades. Using concrete examples from the units of study, we address the five instructional principles (from Chapter 1) in each of the chapters in this section.

The third section (Chapter 6) provides a summary of the main components of disciplinary learning and addresses ways that teachers can design disciplinary literacy instruction in their own classrooms, while ensuring that they have addressed the CCSS and the five instructional design principles we weave throughout the book. This chapter synthesizes the processes we enacted to create disciplinary literacy units and includes practical suggestions for teachers as they develop and enact their own disciplinary literacy instruction.

Acknowledgments

No one can whistle a symphony;
it takes a whole orchestra to play it.
                              —Halford E. Luccock

This book is the result of hundreds of hours of teaching and learning by an extensive network of educational collaborators. First, we thank the wonderful teachers and their students who opened their doors to collaborate with us to design and implement the disciplinary literacy units featured in this book. MaryLiz Magee, Heather Winchester, and Tanya D'Forno invited us into their 2nd-grade classroom in Reno, Nevada, to codevelop and implement the science unit focused on why we care for the air, land, and water. Elisabeth Trost-Shahata and her 4th-grade English learners in Chicago, Illinois, worked with us to codevelop, enact, and write up the unit on why we remember Sacagawea. Cassandra (pseudonym) and her 6th-graders welcomed us into their classroom to codesign and enact the unit on school budgets in Reno, Nevada.

Second, we thank the teacher educators who shared their expertise in a particular discipline. David Crowther, a professor of science education at the University of Nevada, Reno, helped design and implement the unit in MaryLiz's classroom. Julie Pennington, an associate professor of literacy studies who specializes in early literacy at the University of Nevada, Reno, also helped to design and implement the 2nd-grade unit. Kathryn Obenchain, an assistant professor of social studies at Purdue University, taught us about social studies and history, and played a major role in designing the unit in Elisabeth's classroom. Lynda Wiest, a professor of mathematics education at the University of Nevada, Reno, helped design and implement the unit in Cassandra's classroom. The disciplinary experts assisted in writing the classroom example sections of Chapters 2–5. However, their contributions went beyond individual chapters as we integrated what we had learned from our conversations with them across the book in building coherence among chapters. To each of them, we are grateful for their generosity in sharing their expertise. We also thank Jennifer Morrison, who helped with the unit on budgeting in Cassandra's room. She developed Figure 2.5 that we used in Chapter 2.

Additionally, the book's senior authors, Cindy and Ginny, acknowledge specific contributions from Elisabeth, who contributed to our thinking about diverse learners with specific language needs, and Kate, who led the assessment sections. We appreciate Taffy's contributions throughout the writing and revision process. A special thank you to the three book prospectus reviewers who gave us valuable suggestions. Finally, we thank Jean Ward at Teachers College Press. We appreciate her guidance and support throughout the writing process.

NOTE

We acknowledge the Institute of Education Sciences, U.S. Department of Education, Grant R305F100007, to University of Illinois at Chicago, which provided partial support to the third author for her contributions to this collaborative project. The opinions expressed are those of the authors and do not represent views of the Institute or the U.S. Department of Education.

PART I

Setting the Context

The first Part provides an overview of the conceptual content for the rest of the book. In Chapter 1, the introduction, we situate an instructional framework in the current educational context, introduce disciplinary literacy, and discuss its relationship to the CCSS. We also introduce five research-based principles of effective instruction that we weave throughout the remaining chapters in the book. Chapter 2 provides an in-depth examination of disciplinary literacy and why it is important for teaching in elementary classrooms. We briefly introduce readers to the three classrooms (lower, middle, and upper elementary) featured in this book and the disciplinary literacy units we enacted in each class.

CHAPTER 1

Setting the Framework for Instructional Ideas

Virginia Goatley, Taffy Raphael,
and Cynthia Brock

In the second decade of the 21st century, the Common Core State Standards (CCSS) are providing a framework for curriculum and instruction (Common Core State Standards Initiative, 2010). Although these new standards likely mirror some components of existing individual state standards, they offer an opportunity to (re)visit core ideas about English language arts (ELA) education and the key aspects of learning that are important for students to develop throughout their schooling. Some states will not be adopting the CCSS. Those that do may find their enactment of CCSS affected by the assessments under development (PARCC, Smarter Balance). Consequently, our goal is consider how this moment in time reinforces particular research-based practices. In this chapter, we share significant components of the standards and general education principles that guide decisions about curriculum, instruction, and assessment practices.

Drawn from the anchor standards for college and career readiness, the CCSS provide curricular suggestions for kindergarten through 12th grade, building toward what high school graduates should be able to accomplish upon completion of formal schooling. The standards remind us of the need for critical disciplinary learning so that students are engaged in experiences that apply to reading and writing outside of school. As with any set of new educational standards, we need to be both cautious about focusing too much on a narrow interpretation of their meaning and long-term impact (Loveless, 2012; Tucker, 2011), as well as optimistic about the opportunities they might afford (Goatley & Overturf, 2011).

OPPORTUNITIES FOR INSTRUCTIONAL
AND CURRICULAR IMPROVEMENTS

Effective instruction requires teachers to be decisionmakers who continually seek to improve their practice. That is, effective teachers always seek new ideas and opportunities for literacy education. In this section, we share six areas for consideration, opportunities prompted by the CCSS, but stemming from literacy research. These areas provide guidance for instructional priorities, particularly at the elementary level where critical assumptions of reading and writing provide the foundation for secondary schooling.

Expanded Definitions of Literacy

The CCSS emphasize that literacy is a process of high-level thinking and analysis that includes the ability to make claims, warrant the claims, and support them through multiple sources of evidence. This is a welcome change from the legacy of No Child Left Behind with its narrow definition of reading and its limited emphasis on word-level activities. The CCSS shift the focus to students as critical consumers and producers of both reading and writing for real-world purposes. Further, the CCSS encourage us to revisit research in areas such as comprehension, writing, disciplinary learning, and text difficulty to provide a more expansive view of what students need to accomplish (Pearson, 2012).

Technological Visions

With the expanded definition of literacy, the CCSS turn our attention to the materials that comprise the sources for readers in the 21st century, inviting us to consider the technological world in which we live. Watching toddlers engage with iPads or smart phones makes it clear that texts and literacy are evolving quickly; the literacy world of today's youngsters will be very different by the time they graduate high school or college. We need to understand how technologies influence text choices, text genres, interactions with text, and ability to interpret and produce text (Coiro, 2011; Coiro & Dobler, 2007; Sweeney, 2011; Zhang, Duke, & Jimenez, 2011). Then, we can help students assume a critical stance when encountering the range of authors who write text online and in print, while also recognizing the power of their own writing to potentially influence an international audience with the click of a button.

Challenging Curriculum

With changes to the ways that literacy is being defined and enacted, the new standards create an opportunity to consider how we have inadvertently ignored a key element in the curriculum—the need to encourage the use of more complex texts at earlier levels. In doing so, educators will need to address the dual goals of helping students read these complex, age-appropriate texts while also ensuring instruction with texts at students' appropriate instructional reading levels on their way to becoming facile with more complex texts (Hiebert & Sailors, 2009; Raphael, Florio-Ruane, George, Hasty, & Highfield, 2004). Educators will need to determine how to select texts for teacher read-alouds and for reading within teacher-led groups. In short, we must challenge students to meet their potential for learning, while providing effective scaffolding to build students' confidence and interest in learning. Further, we need to maintain and continue to support children in their development of foundational aspects of literacy (National Institute of Child Health and Human Development, 2000), while also seeking a goal toward a much broader definition and enactment of literacy practice.

Text Choices

With curricula that reflect rising expectations come opportunities to expand the choices of texts used as a basis for literacy instruction. Informational texts, poems, stories, biographies, mathematical problems, and so forth are increasingly available at a variety of text levels. We need to think about how to introduce the breadth of the genres available and what these texts "buy us" in terms of new learning opportunities for students (Duke, Caughlin, Juzwik, & Martin, 2012; Maloch & Bomer, 2013). That is, we need to be thoughtful about how we use informational texts, rather than simply increasing the time students have to read them. A criticism of the original list of text exemplars provided in Appendix B of the CCSS is that they do not represent a range of languages and cultures (Boyd, 2012/2013; Goatley, 2011; Sims Bishop, 2011). This reminds us that, as teachers, we must critically read and interpret the CCSS just as we critically read and interpret other important texts. As teachers, we must make sure that students see their own culture represented in literature on current issues and topics, not simply as the historical representations from time periods such as the Civil War or the civil rights movement.

Disciplinary Learning

Beyond their emphasis on different texts, the new standards create opportunities to foreground learning in the disciplines, such as history and science. Elementary school curriculum often neglected this focus on the disciplines during the NCLB era. Educators can build deep knowledge within disciplinary areas through strategic application of ELA tools, as well as help students connect history, mathematics, science, and literature in important and meaningful ways (Moje, Stockdill, Kim, & Kim, 2010). Of course, success in disciplinary learning assumes that educators know how to support students as they explore disciplinary concepts and how genres and text structures vary based on both discipline and intent.

Motivation and Engagement

The CCSS mention the importance of student motivation, but only in terms of matching texts to readers, including "reader variables such as motivation, knowledge and experience" (CCSS, 2010, p. 31). However, there is a large body of scholarship pertaining to motivation that emphasizes the importance of developing curriculum and providing instruction that provides a purpose for, and supports, student learning (Guthrie, Coddington, & Wigfield, 2009; Ozgungor, & Guthrie, 2004). Teachers must take student interest and motivation into account when choosing resources and developing instruction, while also choosing texts and activities that lead students to ideas and concepts they might not choose to explore on their own (Guthrie & Klauda, 2012).

IMPLICATIONS FOR TEACHING PRACTICES

So, now that we have new standards that offer suggestions for shifts in instruction and curriculum, what do they mean for teaching practices? If the goal is for students to graduate from high school able to meet these standards, "without significant scaffolding," then teachers need to consider the nature of support as students learn and as they build their independence. As with any new initiative, there are certainly potential cautions for teachers in enacting instructional practices to address the CCSS, particularly if they are asked to narrow their focus to teach solely to stated standards or to limit what they already know about effective research-based practices. Although standards provide a framework, teachers need to interpret the documents to inform instruction. The CCSS, as with any standards documents, open the door for teaching key concepts and constructs through instructional units designed with the standards in mind. In constructing new units that align with the intent of the CCSS, educators may change how they think about developing reading and writing goals, and how these shifting goals transform the instructional support teachers provide to students. Then, they need to be prepared for tackling instructional challenges that are a component of any new policy.

Developing Critical Reading and Writing Goals

As a field, we have long known that effective readers and writers are those who can engage critically with text as consumers and producers (Elbow, 1998; Graves, 1983; Routman, 2004). There are, and have long been, many paths to accomplish this goal of critical engagement with text. The current CCSS present one important path to address the issue of critical engagement with text by promoting skills in argumentation and effective use of evidence to support a particular position. In short, for students to be successful writers, they need to be able to persuade, to use evidence to support their claims, to evaluate texts in ways that lead them to create effective arguments, and to use writing in an authentic manner. Authenticity of reading and writing is a critical instructional implication of the standards, one that has the potential to engage students in real-world literacy goals.

Literacy educators (e.g., Routman, 2004; Tompkins, 2011) indicate that to be critical consumers and producers of text, students need to learn in ways that make sense to them, and then apply these ideas to real-world uses of writing. For example, they may need to:

- Learn to argue and argue to learn
- Learn to disagree in an agreeable way
- Bring critical analysis to what they read
- Use writing to persuade, both their own ideas and collective positions
- Understand that real writing has power
- Always consider that real writing has an audience

Consistent with the CCSS, an ultimate goal is that "Students can, without significant scaffolding, comprehend and evaluate complex texts across a range of types and disciplines, and they can construct effective arguments and convey intricate or multifaceted information" (CCSS, 2010, p. 7). Such a goal provides an opportunity to shift instruction in elementary schools from solely teaching basic reading and writing skills and strategies to having much higher expectations for teaching students how to develop complex and authentic understandings of texts in real-world contexts.

Tackling Instructional Challenges

When interpreting the standards for instructional implications, we recognize the extensive and significant research about reading and writing instruction that details how students read: drawing on prior knowledge, linking texts to their own experiences and responses, and making sure comprehension is always a focus (Duke & Carlisle, 2010; Snow, Griffin, & Burns, 2005). For example, as students engage in close reading of short texts to learn new information, the background knowledge they bring to interpret and understand remains important. In rereading, we want to encourage them to consider new interpretations and ideas provided by the text.

The teacher plays a critical role in making these instructional decisions to provide extra support for the more challenging ideas and texts associated with the concepts of complex texts and deep learning. In this book, we will address many of the questions we are hearing from teachers around the country as they encounter the CCSS and anticipate the instructional shifts that might occur as teachers implement the CCSS. For example, many elementary teachers know the "Goldilocks" method of text selection—not too easy, not too hard, but just right. The standards are encouraging us to consider not only the traditional benefits of this process but also its limitations (see Fisher, Frey, & Lapp, 2012). Questions that stem from this instructional goal include the following:

- How do we introduce more challenging texts to students who cannot yet read them on their own?
- What is the role of rereading, read-alouds, and vocabulary building in introducing challenging texts?
- Isn't the concept of increasing text complexity at odds with how we support students in reading, building confidence, and increasing motivation? What exactly does it mean?
- What is deep/close reading? How does it impact learning?

While addressing important instructional questions like the ones above, and taking advantage of the new opportunities made available by the adoption of the CCSS, we must also adhere to the instructional principles we know are valuable and critical for supporting student learning.

All students can be successful when the instructional context provides opportunities for teachers to meet what Raphael and her colleagues (Florio-Ruane & Raphael, 2004; Raphael, Florio-Ruane, & George, 2001) term teachers' *dual commitments*. The first commitment is ensuring that students have access to age-appropriate materials, the "complex texts" that are mentioned repeatedly in the CCSS documents. This commitment underscores students' need for opportunities to learn using resources that are written for their age group—even if they need support to read and understand these materials. The second commitment is helping students advance in their reading skills by working with them at their instructional level. This means that students need opportunities to engage with texts that push their reading to increasingly higher levels, using texts that—with guided practice from the teacher—are appropriate to their current reading level. Their current level may be above or below that expected for their age group. These two commitments simply recognize that many students are not able to handle the complexity of texts written for their age group, or may need support in making sense of texts within school subjects such as history and science. Age-appropriate and reading-level-appropriate texts may not be one and the same.

To achieve the intent behind the CCSS and to accelerate learning with the goal of reducing the persistent achievement gap, instruction in the English language arts will need to keep these dual commitments front and center. Students need time daily to engage with both age-appropriate and reading-level-appropriate materials. Learning in disciplinary areas provides authentic purposes for learning and using English language arts in reading (with scaffolding and independently) age-appropriate texts. It also moves instruction from being solely about process to fostering substantive learning about disciplinary content. The units described in Chapters 3–5 illustrate how CCSS can be enacted in the context of meaningful disciplinary study, using complex texts written for the students' age group and texts that support students' learning of conceptual knowledge. The educators created each unit using a set of design principles that ensured that the dual commitments could be met through developmentally appropriate instructional activities using complex texts to explore essential questions. In the next section, we consider how the standards and related implications for teaching lead to creating new curriculum that improves instruction.

CREATING CURRICULUM FOR ELA IN DISCIPLINARY LEARNING:
FIVE DESIGN PRINCIPLES TO IMPROVE INSTRUCTION

As we noted in the first section of the chapter, the CCSS documents help us think about the opportunities the new standards afford, particularly in their emphasis on high-level literate and mathematical thinking. The CCSS underscore the importance of maintaining a rigorous, aligned curriculum across the grade levels to ensure that students are on track to meet the ultimate criteria of being ready for college and career. For teachers in the elementary grades, the new standards provide opportunities to create curriculum that is meaningful to students and that brings excitement into teaching and learning. However, designing such curriculum can be challenging. Enacting these standards involves teachers (on their own, in grade level and cross-disciplinary teams, and as a professional learning community) in the significant work of developing the assessment tools, instructional strategies, and material resources they can use to ensure that their students are on track to success.

The educators contributing to this book took up the challenge of creating meaningful curriculum for elementary grades that was based on five instructional design principles. From kindergarten through intermediate grades, designing instructional units with a strong disciplinary focus raises unique problems. In the balance between instruction in the English language arts and teaching disciplinary learning, the emphasis has historically been on the former. The new standards seek a balance, significantly increasing the emphasis on disciplinary learning and the related need for reading complex texts. Thus, curriculum aligned with CCSS requires a balance between developing a wide repertoire of literacy tools with learning the disciplinary content, and balancing opportunity to continue to teach students at their instructional level, while ensuring that all engage with the complex tests of the disciplines.

The work described in this book reflects the thinking of educational teams that included elementary classroom teachers, disciplinary experts, and university-based colleagues who collaborated to create, enact, and evaluate units that balance and integrate instruction in ELA and disciplinary learning. The teams drew on a set of five research-based design principles in developing the units described in Chapters 3–5. The design principles reflect the opportunities presented in CCSS for becoming literate thinkers within and across disciplines, achieving the vision of an excellent graduating 6th-grader. The principles emphasize the types of contexts and the curriculum content that help teachers meet their dual commitments, doing so through units driven by inquiry into essential questions.

Principle 1: Authentic social and cultural practices are
critical features of instructional units

For decades, scholars (e.g., Barab, Gresalfi, Dodge, & Ingram-Goble, 2010; Graves, 1983; Gutiérrez, 2008; Scribner & Cole, 1981) have argued for the importance of situating learning in authentic social and cultural practices. These practices change across time. For example, Graves's (1983) classic work emphasized authentic writing practice as writing for peers (e.g., Graves & Hansen, 1983; Hansen, 1983), becoming a classroom or school writing community. More recent iterations involve student writers reaching audiences beyond their classrooms through podcasts (Vasinda & McLeod, 2011) or online communities (Larson, 2009).

Authentic practices vary across disciplines, as do the tools required for successful disciplinary learning. As Moje (2010) notes, "there is little research or practical experience with how to *teach* within and across [disciplines] in ways that support a novice's developing competence with more and more sophisticated texts of different domains" (p. 47). The design teams developing the units described in Chapters 3–5 identified authentic practices within their disciplinary focus (e.g., observation in science, mathematical modeling for tracking and prediction) and related tools to support these practices (e.g., the use of observation logs in science, digital spreadsheets for modeling budgets and anticipating expenses in mathematics) that were then woven into the instructional activities of the unit, from initial explanation of the tools to their application during the inquiry activities.

Principle 2: An optimal learning model provides a
framework for instructional units

The concept of an optimal model for learning (Routman, 2003) grows out of the family of developmental theories related to how learners construct knowledge (Vygotsky, 1978). Such a model includes balancing explicit instruction, modeling, coaching, independent practice based on the needs of a disciplinary unit and what students are going to be expected to do. The underlying principle of guided practice, optimal learning, gradual release of responsibility, and other terms familiar to literacy educators is the idea that what an individual learns begins in the social practices guided by the more knowledgeable "other" (e.g., teacher, more experienced peer, tutor, parent). When scholars (e.g., Au & Raphael, 1998; Gavelek & Raphael, 1996; Pearson, 1986; Routman, 2003) have unpacked what this looks like— moving from the interpersonal to the intrapersonal—they have generally agreed on the following components: (1) explicit instruction by the more knowledgeable "other," (2) modeling using strategies such as thinking aloud when what is being modeled cannot be directly observed, (3) guided practice where the teacher and learner jointly work through a task, and (4) independent practice that provides the teacher with information that guides next steps for instruction.

In literacy instruction, this process is often linear from explicit instruction through independent practice and assessment. In disciplinary instruction, however, the components are balanced but not necessarily linear. This balance is reflected in units as teachers use discipline-specific approaches to instruction. For example, in science, primary initial pedagogical approaches include inquiry and open-ended exploration on which later explicit explanations build. Beginning with scientific exploration rather than explanation provides experiences for building background knowledge. The exploration serves as a form of *writing into* a unit as students document their experiences for later examination.

Principle 3: Key inquiry questions give structure to disciplinary study

Researchers have characterized inquiry in terms of thematic study (Lipson, Valencia, Wixson, & Peters, 1993), integrated instruction (Gavelek, Raphael, Biondo, & Wang, 2000), and disciplinary learning (Moje, Stockdill, Kim, & Kim, 2010). In all cases, the goal is better instruction across disciplines, in ways that carefully maintain the integrity of each discipline. Each unit described in Chapters 3–5 focuses on a central inquiry question within science, social studies, or math. For example, the 4th-grade unit explores the question: Why should we remember Sacagawea? Central history concepts addressed across the unit include expedition and exploration, as students explore cultural universals (i.e., the domains of human experience such as food, clothing, and shelter that exist for all cultures), the five themes of geography (i.e., location, place, regions, movement, and human-environment interactions), and historical empathy (i.e., how we, in the present day, can understand and empathize with historical figures from the past).

Principle 4: Composing meaning within and across units requires a range of resources (including both conventional texts and digital media)

Texts sets have been recommended for almost 2 decades (e.g., Ogle, Klemp, & McBride, 2007; Opitz, 1998). Text sets have conventionally consisted of a range of print materials (picture books to chapter books, fiction and nonfiction, magazines) that are linked thematically and represent a range of reading levels. They also reflect a range of levels of text complexity and include literary texts (e.g., fiction, poetry), research materials (e.g., informational texts, newspapers, webpages), and opinion pieces (e.g., editorials, blogs, op-ed pages) (see Ebbers, 2002). Text sets are critically important in meeting dual commitments and are particularly useful in ensuring that students are taught ELA using texts at their instructional level yet, regardless of that level, are able to contribute substantively to disciplinary explorations throughout the unit.

In the units described in Chapters 3–5, the design teams assembled text sets to give students opportunities to learn the 21st-century literacy skills they need for success (see Coiro, 2003; Leu, Kinzer, Coiro, & Cammack, 2004). Coiro (2003) points out that, to some degree, long-known comprehension strategies are relevant even when engaging with media literacies, but although they are related, they require new ways of thinking. For example, the Internet uses hypertext and interactive media that require different ways of understanding from traditional linear texts. Moreover, the Internet provides new ways to acquire knowledge, verify the credibility of sources, and apply what has been learned, as well as new activities for sharing beyond the classroom (e.g., multimedia projects, online communities).

In creating curriculum units that bridged the ELA and disciplinary learning, the design teams considered *how* the different text types would be introduced and used in inquiry and literacy instruction (within the frame of the dual commitments) and how what was learned from these text sets would be applied in practice (reading, writing, and talking about text).

Principle 5: Authentic assessments must reflect the different types of meaning-making processes students use as they read, write, and talk in the course of instruction

Reading and Authentic Assessment. At the elementary level, the CCSS require a shift in orientation that is somewhat more complex than in middle and high school, where a disciplinary focus already dominates. There is a strong theoretical base (Vygotsky, 1978) as well as a broad research base on the importance of early reading instruction (Fountas & Pinnell, 1996; Scanlon, Anderson, & Sweeney, 2010). Guided reading requires that teachers find the right texts (Hiebert & Sailors, 2009) to challenge students to increasingly higher levels of achievement, using texts that, with appropriate support from the teachers, they can read, comprehend, analyze, and critique. Similarly, research on close reading (Greenleaf, Schoenbach, &

Cziko, 2001) documents the ways in which effective teachers use modeling and coaching to support students' reading within disciplinary areas such as literature, history, and science. These bodies of research reflect the teachers' role in meeting the dual commitments of literacy instruction.

While implementing the units, the teachers provided guidance and assessment in guided reading groups, and they used complex disciplinary materials. The contexts for guided reading and assessment are consistent with long-standing practices of grouping students together within a fairly narrow band of reading levels. Central to these units is the use of text sets (Ogle, Klemp, & McBride, 2007) that are thematically connected to the driving inquiry question of the unit. While instruction and assessment using these text sets focuses on developing increasingly higher levels of competence in the English language arts, the content of the material provides those at every reading level with the ability to contribute new information as they engage in inquiry.

The context for close reading of age-appropriate materials can take a variety of forms. In some units, a Book Club model (Goatley, Brock, & Raphael, 1995; Raphael & McMahon, 1994; Raphael, Pardo, & Highfield, 2002) is adapted. In this context, students read texts written for their age level and are supported by teachers in close reading of the texts using a range of pedagogical tools. Support for hearing the oral language of the text can be provided through listening centers/audiobooks, digital books with embedded support, and teacher read-alouds. Support, and ongoing authentic assessment, during close readings emphasizes concept development, text features, structures, vocabulary, background knowledge demands, linguistic understanding, and so forth.

Writing and Authentic Assessment. Writing is a tool central to learning, and elementary school is critical for starting students on a path to using writing comfortably to achieve a range of purposes. Writing experiences provide a way into examining the driving question at the beginning of the unit (e.g., through initial inquiry, connecting to personal experiences), during the unit (e.g., through logs, journals), and at the end of the unit (e.g., reflection, extension activities). The context of interdisciplinary units provides authentic purposes for writing, authentic use of tools for effective communication, authentic assessment of students' writing, and the opportunity to make connections between reading and writing (Routman, 2004). In designing units to address this principle, the teams focused on opportunities for students to engage as critical consumers of the writing of others as well as producers of written text that serve particular purposes within the unit. Instructional support focuses on guiding students to: (1) consider *why* writers write, (2) learn *how* writers write, and (3) use texts in the text set to examine *what writers do* (Routman, 2004). In creating curriculum, the team members identified sites within the units where these constructs can be taught, organizing instructional sites in terms of authentic writing activities *writing into* a unit, activities that help students *writing through* the unit, and activities that lead to looking back at the unit and reflecting as they *write out* of the unit (Raphael et al., 2004).

Activities for *writing into* disciplinary inquiry may involve accessing relevant background knowledge through reflective essays, building background knowledge through mini-reports on key constructs, working with upcoming vocabulary, and so forth. Instructional support for learning by *writing through* the unit focuses on journaling, note-taking, question-asking, and other tools that support information gathering and organizing. Opportunities for instruction as students *write out* of the unit range from creating individual reports (informational writing), creating an argument (claim) and using evidence from the unit to warrant and support the claim, prepare for a debate by addressing the inquiry position from multiple perspectives, and so forth. Throughout the inquiry unit, opportunities exist to use writing, and to assess the use of writing, in both conventional paper-pencil formats (e.g., journals) as well as with digital tools (e.g., mind maps, Excel digital worksheets, podcasts).

Talk and Authentic Assessment. Decades of research on classroom discourse provide unequivocal support on the importance of conversation for learning and undeniable evidence that high-quality talk in classrooms takes many forms. Effective classroom conversation can center on literary discussions (e.g., Book Clubs, described in Raphael et al., 2002; Grand Conversations, described by Eeds & Wells, 1989) that can be student-to-student or teacher-facilitated. Effective discussion involves disciplinary inquiry and exploration (e.g., Wells, 1993). But regardless of the form it takes, effective discussion is goal-directed, is structured, and allows students time to share their thoughts. Such conversations are prompted by authentic questions that tend to invite longer contributions from students and greater elaboration of their ideas. These, in turn, tend to encourage reasoning and higher levels of thinking (Soter et al., 2008).

In designing the units described in Chapters 3–5, a variety of contexts for productive talk were created and assessed, from dyads discussing data collected to small-group discussions of literature and inquiry project information to teacher-led whole-group discussions of read-alouds and formal presentations.

CONCLUDING COMMENTS

Standards have been enacted in many states since the 1980s and, since 2003, in all states. Looking at evidence to date, the Brown Center Report on American Education (Loveless, 2012) concluded that, "The empirical evidence suggests that the Common Core will have little effect on American students' achievement. The nation will have to look elsewhere for ways to improve its schools" (p. 14). Although we agree that standards alone cannot lead to sustainable improvements, the rhetorical power and policies that stem from standards—especially nationally supported ones such as CCSS—do impact the day-to-day lives of teachers and students. The CCSS are standards that provide an opportune moment in educational reform for teachers to teach in ways that *can*—though, of course, are not guaranteed to—lead to learning. What a joy to be mandated to teach to high levels of thinking, prepare our students for a lifetime of success and personal satisfaction, engage in interesting work to learn about the physical and social world, and engage with one another in debate, argumentation, and persuasion using what was learned through their exploration of new content.

CHAPTER 2

Disciplinary Literacy in Elementary Classrooms

Cynthia Brock, Virginia Goatley,
Taffy Raphael, and Elisabeth Trost-Shahata

In this chapter, we delve deeper into the meaning of disciplinary literacy. First, we explore four problems related to teaching disciplinary literacy in elementary classrooms. Second, we introduce three teachers and their classrooms featured in Chapters 3, 4, and 5. Third, we describe the units these three teachers have created to teach disciplinary literacy effectively, contrasting them with a "non-example" from a classroom where disciplinary literacy instruction is less effective.

We ask you questions throughout the book to help facilitate your thinking while engaging with the ideas we present. For this chapter, think about how you define disciplinary literacy. How does disciplinary literacy influence your instruction in science, math, and history?

INTRODUCING AND CONTEXTUALIZING DISCIPLINARY LITERACY

Because No Child Left Behind's policies focused on English language arts (ELA) and mathematics instruction, science and social studies instruction for elementary school children was marginalized or even, in some cases, eliminated (Kinniburgh & Busby, 2008; VanFossen, 2005). The adoption of the Common Core State Standards (CCSS, or Common Core) has led most states in the United States to turn their attention to the disciplines (Calkins, Ehrenworth, & Lehman, 2012; Goatley, 2012; Neuman & Gambrell, 2013; Pearson, 2013). This shift has heightened teachers' need to understand how reading, writing, and talk can be used as tools to learn and understand the disciplines. As we explore the role of ELA in disciplinary teaching and learning, we begin by considering four central problems for implementing disciplinary literacy instruction in the elementary grades.

Problem 1: Limited research base on disciplinary literacy in elementary grades. What does disciplinary literacy look like in elementary classrooms? Teachers at the elementary level have scant research on which to base their disciplinary literacy instruction (Moje, 2007) since research has focused primarily on middle and high school levels (e.g., Draper, 2008; Moje, 2007; Shanahan & Shanahan, 2008). Yet, disciplinary literacy foundations built in elementary grades are critical to the successful use of literacy to foster disciplinary learning in upper grades (National Council of Teachers of English, 2011).

As educators, we find ourselves in a dilemma because the elementary grades have lacked the extended time, energy, and research on the disciplines that characterize middle school and secondary levels. The NCLB focus on reading and mathematics led some states to suspend or eliminate social studies and science assessments (e.g., New York State Education Department, 2010). The NCLB message was clear—educational policymakers minimally valued disciplinary learning in the elementary grades, creating a domino effect. High-stakes assessments in reading and mathematics, with no assessment in other disciplines, promoted minimal disciplinary instruction (Pace, 2007; Wills, 2007). The adoption of the Common Core has brought us to a pivotal juncture regarding disciplinary instruction in elementary schools. The emphasis that policymakers are placing on disciplinary learning provides elementary teachers the license to allocate significant instructional time to it. Since elementary and secondary contexts vary considerably, however, we cannot simply import secondary research into elementary classrooms. We have reached a crossroads where we now need to reenvision, reimagine, and innovate disciplinary instruction and research in elementary schools.

When we consider the amount of coursework that elementary teachers have in the disciplines and the sheer number of disciplines an elementary teacher is responsible for teaching, we need to ensure that they have the knowledge needed to teach disciplinary content. Supporting elementary teachers to be well prepared and engaged in ongoing learning is critical, given the limited research on disciplinary literacy for elementary teachers and the recognition that these teachers are the primary teachers of the disciplines.

Problem 2: Disciplinary literacy in the elementary grades is minimally defined. How do you define disciplinary literacy? The common distinction between "learning to read" (usually associated with K–3) and "reading to learn" (usually associated with 4th grade and beyond) meant disciplinary learning was historically not emphasized until the upper elementary grades. However, this delay presents three concerns. First, research on the role of background knowledge in comprehending text indicates that children bring their knowledge to bear as they read. Even very young children have developing conceptual understandings that intertwine with their reading development (Dyson, 2003). Second, research on motivation and engagement (Guthrie, Wigfield, & Humenick, 2006; Mohr, 2006) indicates that young children have strong interests in discipline-related topics (e.g., birds, dinosaurs, space). Effective instruction needs to capitalize on those interests through texts used to teach reading (Allington & Gabriel, 2012; Duke, 2004). Third, some children in upper elementary grades still struggle with reading and writing. These children continue to need supportive literacy interventions while they are learning the disciplines (Herman & Wardrip, 2012). Thus, children and adolescents are best served when engaged in disciplinary instruction while simultaneously learning to read and write throughout their elementary years and beyond.

The Common Core also indicates that children should be learning the disciplines at a younger age. What does this mean for defining and enacting disciplinary literacy in elementary school? A major focus of disciplinary literacy is how to use literacy to engage in the thinking associated with conceptual knowledge in the disciplines. Shanahan and Shanahan (2008) use the term *disciplinary literacy* to refer to the literacy skills specialized to subjects such as history, science, mathematics, and literature. Moje (2008) further suggests that a focus on disciplinary literacy requires a curriculum in which "young people learn how to access, interpret, challenge, and reconstruct the texts of the discipline . . . [as] accepted practice" (p. 100).

Current conceptions of disciplinary literacy may best be understood by contrasting them with their antecedent, *content area literacy*. Historically, researchers such as Herber (1970), Anders and Guzetti (1996), and Alvermann and Swafford (1989) provided detailed insights into *content area reading* strategies, where teachers (often preservice teachers learning to be content specialists) learned a set of generic literacy strategies that they could apply to their respective disciplines. The key distinction between content area literacy and disciplinary literacy is that content area literacy started with generic literacy strategies, and secondary teachers (often inexperienced preservice teachers) determined how to apply them to their unique disciplines. Disciplinary literacy, in contrast, starts with content knowledge and the disciplines themselves by asking educators to consider how to teach reading, writing, and talking as tools, similar to the way disciplinary experts use these tools. The teacher's goal is to use reading, writing, and talking with her students in those unique ways to teach them the content and discourse of the disciplines (Greenleaf, Cribb, Howlett, & Moore, 2010).

How and why did the field move from content area literacy to disciplinary literacy, and what are the implications of this shift for the elementary level? Scholars (e.g., Draper, 2008; Moje, 2007; Shanahan & Shanahan, 2008) began to explore the specific ways that disciplinary experts use reading, writing, and talking as tools in their work. This scholarship prompted the field to shift from content area instruction with its emphasis on the process of instruction through *strategy use* to a greater focus on the *content* of the disciplines and the ways that literacy can be used as a tool to foster disciplinary understandings. Given that most scholarship on disciplinary literacy has occurred at the secondary level (Shanahan & Shanahan, 2012), however, questions emerge about what disciplinary literacy looks like at the elementary level. Worth considering is how disciplinary literacy might be related to older conceptions of thematic or integrated instruction at the elementary level.

Do you remember learning about thematic or integrated instruction? In the past, these concepts often counted as disciplinary instruction. In elementary schools, reading and writing in content areas traditionally occurred within thematic units or inquiry-based instruction (Lipson, Valencia, Wixson, & Peters, 1993; Walmsley, 1994). For example, teachers developed thematic units about family traditions that included literature from various countries and personal connections to the culture. This approach was helpful in many ways, but the primary focus was on literacy, not disciplinary learning. Although thematic units were a good starting point, they are insufficient for teaching the skills and strategies necessary to engage in disciplinary learning (Lipson, Valencia, Wixson, & Peters, 1993). Elementary teachers need to teach disciplinary content as well as literacy-related processes. The shift to incorporating disciplinary literacy at the elementary level provides important opportunities for reenvisioning how and when we teach children to use reading, writing, and talking in ways that are specific to the disciplines.

Problem 3: Elementary children have little experience with informational text. The past decade has unequivocally documented the limited amount of time children spend reading informational texts in elementary classrooms (Duke, 2000; Jeong, Gaffney, & Choi, 2010). Sadly, while researchers point to positive trends in the past 10 years, increasing the amount of time, it is of little practical importance—3.6 seconds to 1 minute in 1st grade, and 16 minutes in 3rd and 4th grade. Not a good situation!

If you think about the informational texts you read aloud in your classroom, what is the typical content? Interestingly, Yopp and Yopp (2012) found that an overwhelming 85% of informational text read-aloud was on science content, compared with 12% for social studies, 2% for language arts, and 1% for mathematics. Even within the science texts, they discovered that 75% focused on topics related to life sciences, leading to minimal exposure to other science areas (e.g., physics, astronomy, geology). Yopp and Yopp noted, "We must be attentive to not only the number, but also the breadth of the informational texts to which we expose children" (p. 484). When children are neither reading informational texts nor seeing them as mentor texts, it negatively impacts their ability to comprehend or create such texts. This is particularly worrisome given the growth of digital media with the related expansion of informational texts and the need for children to be able to read such information critically.

The limited amount of informational text reading in elementary classrooms is exacerbated by the traditional overemphasis on fiction, specifically stories (see Figure 2.1). Although not exhaustive, Figure 2.1 provides types of texts children should encounter consistently in the elementary grades. However, all of these types are critical to consider when planning effective instruction that emphasizes reading, writing, and talking as tools for disciplinary learning. In short, when planning for effective disciplinary literacy instruction, teachers should: (1) use an array of texts, (2) use texts that reflect the full range of genres and purposes as described in Figure 2.1, and (3) be careful to teach critical reading skills not only for current texts, but for effective use of non-refereed information such as that found on the Internet, Facebook, and Twitter.

Problem 4: Norms of the disciplines—how experts think, act, talk, and write within their disciplines—have not been foregrounded in elementary classrooms. Think about how and what you teach in science, math, or history. Scholars in the disciplines write about ways that literacy is central to helping children learn conceptual content (Beauchamp, Kusnick, & McCallum, 2011; Benjamin, 2011; Linder, 2011; Wineburg, 2011). From a science perspective, Steve Metz (2012) reminds science teachers that scientific inquiry both begins and ends with literacy—through reading literature relevant to the scientific concepts and communicating results to others. That is, many disciplinary scholars recognize the ways in which literacy is interwoven throughout their disciplinary work, supporting conceptual learning.

Figure 2.1. Examples of Text Variety

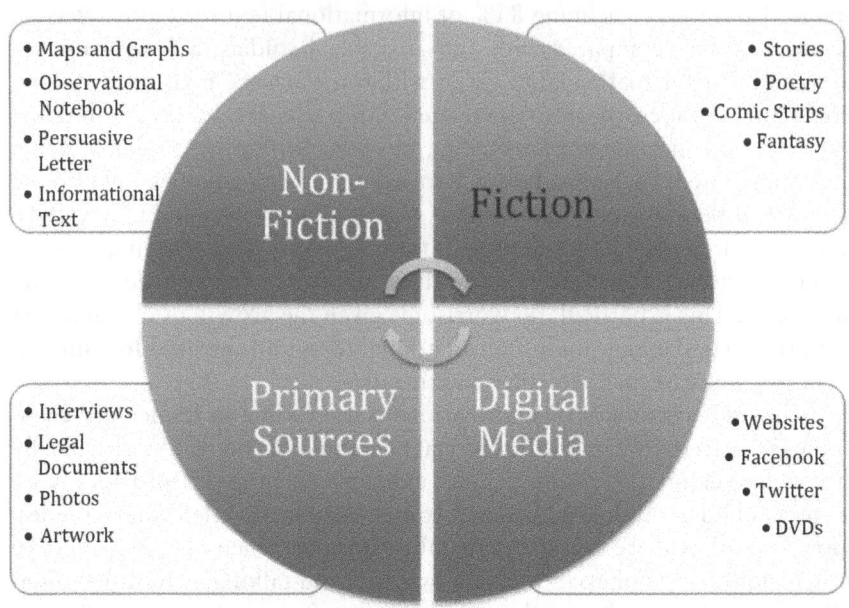

Let's take one concept—argumentation, a component of the Common Core—to explore its different uses across disciplines. For science, Metz (2013) describes argumentation as follows:

> The everyday arguments of children, politicians, and sports fans attempt to win over the opponent, to convince an antagonist that your position is right and the other wrong. In contrast, the goal of argumentation in science is quite the opposite: to reach consensus in a collaborative search for truth. Scientists constantly critique each other's ideas, defend claims and challenge inferences, propose alternative interpretations, and engage in the back-and-forth debate that moves forward our understanding of the natural world. (p. 6)

Other writers (e.g., Llewellyn, 2013; Sampson, Enderle, & Grooms, 2013) make similar points; in science, the role of argument is to build consensus. In her discussion of math classrooms, Cross (2009) emphasizes the importance of argumentation for justifying mathematical ideas. In a study with 9th-graders, Cross (2009) found that students who engaged in both argumentation and mathematical thinking and activities performed better on assessments of knowledge growth than students who engaged in only one or in neither. In social studies (which encompasses several disciplines such as history, economics, and geography), Nussbaum (2002) notes the centrality of argumentation for persuasion. Citizens need to be able to formulate persuasive arguments presenting reasons and evidence for claims. Argumentation is an important concept across these disciplines, but the nature of argumentation varies by discipline (e.g., consensus in science, justification in math, and persuasion in social studies).

NEW CONCEPTIONS OF DISCIPLINARY LITERACY

So, how do we go about implementing disciplinary literacy concepts in our classrooms? Research shows that the ability to provide effective disciplinary literacy instruction requires extensive planning, disciplinary content knowledge, and pedagogical content knowledge (Draper, 2008; Shanahan & Shanahan, 2008; Shulman, 1986). Enacting disciplinary literacy instruction at the elementary level presents unique challenges because: (1) teachers at the elementary level are rarely disciplinary content specialists, and (2) without both disciplinary expertise and a deep understanding of literacy skills and strategies, it is difficult for teachers to know which literacy skills and strategies are most appropriate for each discipline (Shanahan & Shanahan, 2008).

As you move to the next section, keep in mind that we wrote and designed this book with a key goal in mind—to show how to use literacy as a tool to foster disciplinary understandings in the elementary grades. Disciplinary literacy instruction in the elementary grades must foreground the norms of the disciplines in terms of how disciplinary experts think, act, talk, and write. We know this is not easy! In the following section, we introduce you to three teachers who are in the process of sorting through these issues. As you read about them in this and subsequent chapters, consider how they (1) worked to expand their own disciplinary background knowledge and continually engage children in ways that expand their background knowledge of conceptual issues in the disciplines, (2) explored which literacy skills and strategies apply across all disciplines and which are best employed in unique ways in each discipline (Moje, 2007; Shulman, 1986; Wineburg, 2001), and (3) engaged in collaborative work with others, including disciplinary colleagues, grade-level peers, and online forums (e.g., http://www.literacyinlearningexchange.org), to develop systems for building expertise in grade-level disciplinary content.

INTRODUCING MARY, ELISABETH, AND CASSANDRA

In this book, we share practical examples of disciplinary literacy in classroom practice. We drew together three professional learning communities of practitioners who sought to address many of the problems introduced in the previous section. The three teachers, at 2nd, 4th, and 6th grade, represent thoughtful, reflective practitioners interested in understanding how to use literacy as a tool to teach disciplinary understandings. Prompted in part by Common Core, Mary (grade 2), Elisabeth (grade 4), and Cassandra (grade 6) started exploring ways to engage students in effective disciplinary literacy instruction. Throughout this book, we describe how these teachers experimented with disciplinary literacy instruction. We discuss the strengths in their work and challenges they faced, illustrating instructional practices they found useful, as well as instructional practices they plan to modify in future iterations.

Of the many disciplines taught in school, we focus on science, mathematics, and history. The three provide useful points of connection as well as contrast in using reading, writing, and talk as tools for disciplinary learning. Each teacher participated on a collaborative team including a disciplinary and, in one case, a literacy expert. Figure 2.2 displays the grade level, discipline, and guiding inquiry question for each disciplinary literacy unit. We discussed Mary's 2nd-grade science unit in Chapters 4 and 5 of this book, Elisabeth's 4th grade history unit in Chapters 3 and 5, and Cassandra's 6th-grade mathematics unit in Chapters 3 and 4.

Figure 2.3 provides an overview of the teachers and students in three classrooms: (1) Mary's 2nd-grade classroom in a Title I school in Reno, Nevada; (2) Elisabeth's 4th-grade English language learner (ELL) classroom in Chicago, Illinois; and (3) Cassandra's 6th-grade classroom in a Title I school in Reno, Nevada. The three teachers' classrooms were similar in three ways: (1) large class sizes, (2) children predominantly from low-income communities, and (3) most of the students were English learners. Figure 2.3 provides a quick-glance reference for your use as you read subsequent chapters.

EXAMPLES OF DISCIPLINARY LITERACY

In addition to Mary, Elisabeth, and Cassandra, we introduce a fourth teacher, Vivian, in this section only. First, we present two contrasting examples of 4th-grade units of instruction on history—one in Elisabeth's room and

Figure 2.2. Introduction of the Disciplinary Units

Teacher	Mary	Elisabeth	Cassandra
Grade	2nd	4th	6th
Discipline	Science	History	Mathematics
Guiding Inquiry Question	How do we care for our soil, land, and water?	Why do we remember Sacagawea?	How do we make decisions about educational budgets and budgeting in our school district and our school?
Featured Chapters	Chapter 4: Writing Chapter 5: Talk	Chapter 3: Reading Chapter 5: Talk	Chapter 3: Reading Chapter 4: Writing
Disciplinary Expert	Dr. David Crowther and Dr. Julie Pennington	Dr. Kathryn Obenchain	Dr. Lynda Wiest

one in Vivian's room. Juxtaposing an example of disciplinary literacy in Elisabeth's room with a non-example from Vivian's room helps to highlight key features of disciplinary literacy instruction. Second, we present the two remaining examples of disciplinary literacy instruction—one in Mary's 2nd-grade classroom, and one in Cassandra's 6th-grade classroom. As you read through the four classroom examples that follow, ask yourself what you notice about how the teachers use reading, writing, and talking as tools to explore disciplinary content.

Classroom Example 1: Elisabeth, 4th Grade, Social Studies

Elisabeth posed the following question to her 29 4th-grade students: "What do you know about Sacagawea, Thomas Jefferson, and Lewis and Clark?" Elisabeth and her 4th-graders were about to embark on an exciting learning journey. She knew that by the end of the 3-week unit, the students would learn a great deal about social studies concepts and how historians do their work, while building knowledge about Sacagawea, Jefferson, Lewis, and Clark. Elisabeth incorporated historical thinking into the unit by having students consider historical evidence and make interpretations based on

Figure 2.3. Profiles of Classrooms

MARY'S 2ND-GRADE CLASSROOM

- Title I school in Reno, Nevada
- 31 children total
- 4 receive pull-out ESL support
- 21 Latino English learners, 2 African American, 2 Tongan, 6 European American

ELISABETH'S 4TH-GRADE CLASSROOM

- ESL classroom in Chicago, Illinois
- 29 children total, all English learners
- 27 children receive free lunch
- 4 academic groups:

  ➤ 6 newcomers to the United States (from Vietnam, India, Ethiopia, Mexico, and Iraq), beginning to learn English
  ➤ 6 children born in United States, receiving pull-out academic support with special education teacher (Indian, Vietnamese, and Mexican descent)
  ➤ 9 children struggling with literacy, but receiving academic support services (8 from Mexico, 1 from Pakistan)
  ➤ 8 children engaging successfully with English with appropriate instructional support (3 from Mexico, 3 from India, 2 from Iraq)

CASSANDRA'S 6TH-GRADE CLASSROOM

- Title I school in Reno, Nevada
- Most children attended school since kindergarten
- 29 children total
- 19 children are Latino with Spanish as first language, 1 African American, 4 Tongan, 5 European American
- No children receive ESL, 2 receive special education support, three-fifths of children in Cassandra's classroom read at or above grade level

---

that evidence. In contrast to some other historical groups, Elisabeth wanted her students to understand that we do not have much written evidence from Native Americans, like Sacagawea, because historically many Native American cultures had oral traditions. The evidence we do have is written from the perspective of people outside the Native American culture. When historians write about figures such as Sacagawea, they have to frame their interpretations in terms of the perspectives of a White man (e.g., Lewis's journals) writing about a Native American woman rather than how a Native American woman might write about her own experiences. In addition to exploring historical thinking, Elisabeth helped her students explore social studies concepts of expedition, exploration, and movement along with learning about cultural universals. She fostered historical empathy in her students as they worked to increase their historical understanding of Sacagawea, Lewis, and Clark within their time and place in history.

Classroom Example 2: Vivian, 4th Grade, Social Studies

Vivian is a 4th-grade teacher in a small town in Oregon. Twenty-two 4th-graders are in her classroom; 19 are European American and speak English as their first language. Three students are Latino, but speak both Spanish and English fluently. Thus, in contrast to the other three classrooms, less English learners were present.

When the state of Oregon celebrated the sesquicentennial of the Oregon Trail, teachers all over the state spent extra time teaching their students about this historic event. Vivian was no exception. Her students engaged in a myriad of activities to help them understand the history associated with the Oregon Trail. For example, Vivian used many read-alouds of both narrative and informational books about the Oregon Trail. Her students each built a model Calistoga Wagon and created artifacts to include that people traveling the Oregon Trail would likely have taken with them on their journeys. Then, Vivian strung a wire across the classroom and hung the wagons in a row to simulate the wagons traveling in a line across the west. Vivian made a map covering an entire classroom wall showing the Oregon Trail and major landmarks and features along the entire trail from Kansas City, Missouri, to Oregon City, Oregon. Vivian invited guest speakers with expertise about the Oregon Trail to come to speak with her students. One guest even taught the students to make "typical" food eaten by travelers on the Oregon Trail. The principal was so impressed with Vivian's Oregon Trail unit that he invited a reporter from the local newspaper to write a story about Vivian and her students.

* * *

What did you notice about the nature of Elisabeth's and Vivian's instruction? One illustrates disciplinary literacy, while the other does not. If you take a quick look back to Elisabeth's classroom example, you will notice key historical ideas that help illustrate instruction in this classroom: historical thinking, historical evidence, historical empathy, cultural universals, and so forth. In contrast, although Vivian is clearly using engaging activities with her students, her unit focused solely on helping students learn facts about the

Oregon Trail. Moreover, it isn't clear how students would learn to connect these facts conceptually or relate them to one another. In Elisabeth's room, students learned about Sacagawea, Lewis, Clark, and Jefferson; however, *they were learning this information in conjunction with learning about social studies concepts and historical thinking.* For example, Elisabeth taught her students how historians explore historical events; she discussed what counts as historical evidence and how historians make interpretations based on that evidence. In addition, Elisabeth focused on the historical concepts of expedition, exploration and movement, cultural universals, and how these were exemplified in key players in that era.

In short, Elisabeth used her unit to teach her students how historians *do* history (Levstik & Barton, 2010); consequently, rather than coming away from the unit with facts about Sacagawea's life, Elisabeth's students came away from the unit learning what it means to think and act like a historian. She expects and guides them to apply these skills of *doing history* in other social studies units and historical texts both in and out of school. Moreover, Elisabeth uses literacy as a tool to help her students *do* history. In Chapters 3 and 5 of this book, we provide much more information about Elisabeth's work and how she taught her students to use literacy as a tool to *do* history.

As you have likely discerned, Elisabeth's instruction illustrates disciplinary literacy in history. We introduce two additional classroom examples—science in Mary's 2nd-grade classroom and math in Cassandra's 6th-grade classroom—to provide an opportunity for comparing and contrasting the role of ELA as tools in disciplinary learning across fields.

Classroom Example 3: Mary, 2nd Grade, Science

In Figure 2.4, Aneesa, Rochelle, Jose, and Miguel—children in Mary's 2nd-grade classroom—are exploring differences between living and nonliving things. These children are engaged in an inquiry-based unit focusing on environmental stewardship. Across lessons in the unit, they learned about scientific concepts, including habitats and living things, relationships between habitats and living things, and human impact on the environment (e.g., effects of pollution). Children engaged in scientific practices such as observing using words, numbers, and drawings, as well as discerning observable patterns to predict future events.

Mary followed the guidelines of the New Science Framework K–12 (National Research Council, 2012), the guiding document for the Next Generation Science Standards (NGSS Lead States, 2011), to plan her instruction. She concentrated her instruction specifically on Domain 3: Life Science

Figure 2.4. 2nd-Grade Science Observations

Ecosystems: Interactions, Energy, and Dynamics. She also focused on developing Domain 1: Scientific and Engineering Practices. Mary's students enacted these content and process standards by (1) asking questions, (2) conducting investigations, (3) analyzing and interpreting data, (4) constructing explanations, and (5) engaging in discussions based on evidence collected with peers. Throughout this unit, Mary fostered a positive disposition of stewardship toward our environment while using reading, writing, and talking as tools to enact scientific practices as students engaged with life sciences content.

Classroom Example 4: Cassandra, 6th Grade, Mathematics

"How many of you have heard about the potential budget cuts to our local school district?" asked Cassandra. Hands shot up. Questioning further, Cassandra asked, "What have you heard?"

Snippets of what the 6th-graders in Cassandra's class had heard included the following: Jose heard that some schools may be closing, Brisa heard that some teachers would likely lose their jobs or be transferred to different schools, and Juan was concerned that athletics would be cut. After listening to what the children already knew about the budget situation relative to their school district, Cassandra told the children that they would be spending the next few weeks learning more about the budget crisis in their state and its impact on them in their district and their local school. Striving to make her instruction meaningful to her students, Cassandra taught about topics and issues relevant to her students and their community.

* * *

Figure 2.5 provides a conceptual overview of Cassandra's unit. Cassandra began by having the children engage in various lessons that built their background knowledge about national, state, district, and school budgets and budgeting. Interwoven with these lessons, Cassandra used children's literature to teach her children about point of view and persuasion. After building conceptual background knowledge about these topics, students began writing persuasive letters to an official of their choice (e.g., superintendent, governor). In the letters, students expressed their views about the educational budget crisis and made suggestions for how to deal with it effectively in their district and school.

The tenets of quantitative literacy served as the foundation of Cassandra's work with her students. Quantitative literacy "involves knowing how to

Figure 2.5. Conceptual Overview of Budget Unit

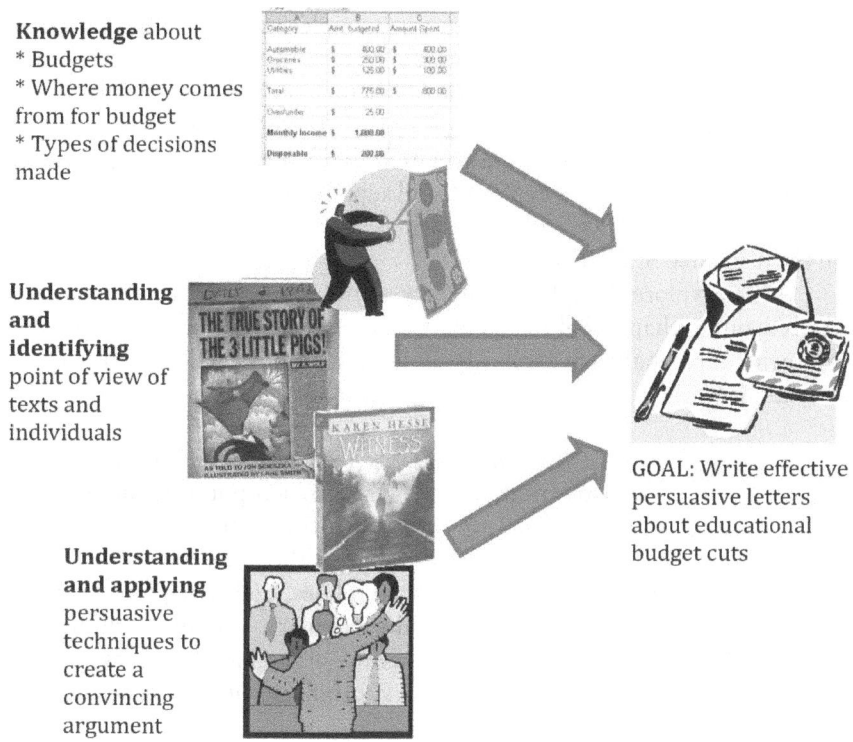

GOAL: Write effective persuasive letters about educational budget cuts

apply essential mathematics skills broadly across varied real-world situations rather than building hierarchical abstract knowledge without regard for meaningful applications" (Wiest, Higgins, & Frost, 2007, p. 48). In particular, Cassandra taught her students concepts that would assist them in learning how mathematicians think, write, and talk about statistical and probabilistic knowledge and reasoning—especially in terms of data representation and interpretation in graphs (Wiest et al., 2007). She also taught her students to do thoughtful Internet research. Cassandra taught her students to develop informed opinions by engaging in the process of data collection, evaluation, and use pertaining to school budgets and budgeting. Cassandra's unit is in alignment with much of the Common Core, particularly in writing a persuasive letter in which the students make and support a claim with relevant details from multiple texts.

CONCLUDING COMMENTS

Across the three disciplinary classroom examples in this chapter, Elisabeth, Mary, and Cassandra actively engaged their students in reading, writing, and talk to develop and extend their disciplinary conceptual knowledge. Consistent with Common Core expectations, these teachers asked students to make observations, gather information, write about their insights on the conceptual processes they explored, and support their new ideas with details from their learning. In the three situations, students were learning to engage in the discourse of the disciplines.

As we explore disciplinary literacy at the elementary level throughout the remaining chapters of this book, we discuss and return repeatedly to the following three main assertions about disciplinary instruction in the elementary grades:

1. *The "Why" of Disciplinary Literacy:* The disciplines need to be the forefront of instruction, not relegated to incorporating the content via literacy instruction (e.g., using historical fiction).
2. *The "What" of Disciplinary Literacy:* Although there are overlapping features across the disciplines, each discipline has its own unique content, norms, and vocabulary. Reading, writing, and talking are tools used to engage in the disciplines. Students need to learn the content, norms, and vocabulary within and across disciplines.
3. *The "How" of Disciplinary Literacy:* Students need to learn to read, write, and discuss a wide variety of genres and forms for different purposes and audiences. To meaningfully teach within the disciplines, educators need to know about relevant genres, forms, audiences, and purposes, and they need to know how to teach across a range of forms and purposes.

PART II

Windows into Classroom Teaching and Learning

Part II draws on the three classrooms introduced in Chapter 2. These three chapters provide vivid windows into classroom teaching and learning showing how reading (Chapter 3), writing (Chapter 4), and talk (Chapter 5) serve as tools to foster disciplinary learning across the elementary grades. Using concrete examples from the units of study, we address the five instructional principles (from Chapter 1) in each of the chapters in this section. We also introduce instructional components particularly relevant to each literacy area essential to teaching the disciplines.

Windows into Classroom Teaching and Learning

CHAPTER 3

Reading Within and Across Texts

Cynthia Brock, Lynda Wiest, Virginia Goatley, Taffy Raphael,
Elisabeth Trost-Shahata, and Catherine Weber

In this chapter, think about two questions—one about you as a reader, and one about you as a teacher of reading. First, have you ever reflected on what occurs as you read? Second, have you ever considered your own beliefs about reading and the role your beliefs play in your decisions about teaching reading? In this chapter, we explore both questions as they relate to reading's role in teaching students conceptual aspects of the disciplines. To help you create effective disciplinary reading instruction in your classroom, we provide examples of how Elisabeth and Cassandra use reading as a tool to teach social studies and mathematics. Figure 3.1 describes disciplinary reading instruction in terms of the Core Design Principles described in Chapter 1.

WHAT MATTERS ABOUT READING INSTRUCTION

What happens when readers read? And, what should we do as teachers to facilitate reading in different disciplines? In this chapter, we present five components of a coherent instructional framework for fostering disciplinary reading. These components describe knowledge of: (1) the reading context, (2) the comprehension process, (3) students as individuals and literacy learners, (4) texts and text features, and (5) disciplinary instructional practices and assessment. First, Figure 3.2 provides an overview of these five components, displaying the overall context in which reading occurs. Second, we discuss each component of the reading process, in turn, elaborating on how the components are interrelated.

Figure 3.1. Core Design Principles in Reading

DESIGN PRINCIPLE	EXAMPLE
1. Authentic Social and Cultural Practices	Use reading as a tool to engage in discipline-specific reading practices (e.g., history-specific reading practices such as using multiple sources to construct an initial interpretation of an event)
2. Optimal Learning Model	Use appropriate scaffolding to help children to develop new conceptual understandings—such as developing historical empathy in history or learning to analyze, interpret, and communicate about data in real-world contexts
3. Key Inquiry Questions	Use inquiry to drive questioning and research to learn new concepts (e.g., to develop understandings of historical events, to understand budgets, and so forth)
4. Composing Requires a Range of Resources	Teach children to draw on resources such as read-alouds, artifacts, Internet research, and interviews with experts in their reading
5. Authentic Assessments Reflect Meaning-Making Process	Use anecdotal notes to monitor the nature of children's reading as they engage with discipline-specific texts

Figure 3.2. Important Components in the Reading Process

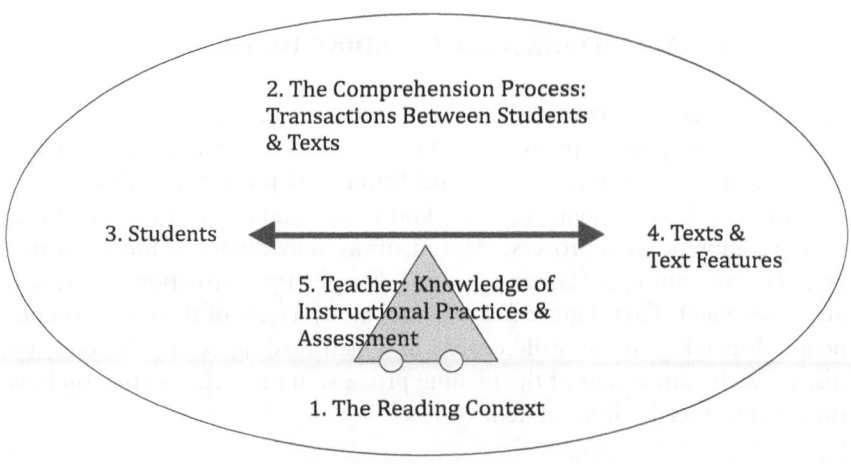

36

Component One: The Reading Context

Teachers need to understand social, cultural, and historical contexts where reading occurs. Do you read all books the same way? For example, are you reading this book the same way you might read a novel at the beach? Reading is not a generic act. Instead, readers in different contexts read differently, depending on the norms in their unique contexts (Design Principle 1). To illustrate this point, it is helpful to consider what researchers have learned about different reading practices across disciplines. For example, Shanahan and Shanahan (2008) found that there are differences in how experts in various disciplines read, and these differences stem from the unique features and contexts of each discipline. For example, they showed that mathematicians used rereading and close reading as the two most important reading approaches. The primary work of mathematicians is to write mathematical proofs. Consequently, it makes sense that they would read and reread texts closely because every word and symbol in a proof matters.

Chemists attend to relationships between written text and diagrams, formulas, and charts. So, as they read, chemists refer back and forth between these written texts and text features in order to understand scientific concepts. Chemists engage in experiments. The write-up of experiments often includes the use of diagrams, formulas, and charts. Consequently, it is logical that chemists read back and forth between written words and different text features.

When historians read, they do not "read the text as truth" (Shanahan & Shanahan, 2008, p. 50). Rather, historians recognize that authors have their own biases and perspectives, so they seek to understand writers' biases and perspectives. Historians analyze historical documents in their work. They interpret historical events based on their analyses of documents and artifacts related to historical events. It stands to reason that they would question writers' biases and perspectives since different documents and artifacts can be analyzed in different ways relative to an historical event.

In sum, the social and cultural context of "reading" depends on how words (written or spoken) are used and interpreted. Readers in different contexts read different kinds of texts in unique ways. Readers need to be taught to understand ways that experts write and interpret different *kinds of texts* (Fang & Schleppegrell, 2010; Moje, 2008).

Component Two: Knowledge of the Comprehension Process

Comprehension occurs in the transaction between students and texts. There is a long, distinguished, and debated history of scholarship about comprehension and the comprehension process, with a current model featured in Figure 3.2. Much of this debate centers on where "meaning" resides when we read. As educators sort out how to implement the Common Core, you will encounter terms such as *close reading* and *text complexity* that place center stage this debate about where meaning resides. For example, one group of educators called "New Critics"—whose ideas were prevalent from the early 1900s to the 1970s—argued that readers derive meaning from text by focusing on the words on the page (Fish, 1982). The principle idea is that "meaning" is located primarily in the words on the page. A second group of scholars called "romantic intentionalists" claims that meaning derives from understanding an author's intentions (including her purposes, goals, and life history) as well as the social, cultural, and historical context in which the text was written (Dutton, 1987). A third group of scholars, called "reader response theorists," argues that meaning is not *in* the words on the page. Rather, meaning is made as a result of the *transaction between* a reader and the text (Rosenblatt, 1938, 2005). The reader brings background experiences and knowledge to her reading of a text, but the text she is reading also constrains the possible interpretations she can make during reading.

Does one of the approaches we just discussed make the most sense to you? If so, it likely influences your instructional decisions. For example, if you believe that meaning resides in the text, you will likely place high value on instruction on the words of the text. If you believe that meaning resides primarily in the author's biography, intentions, and social, cultural, and historical context, you will likely place high value on teaching students about the author and the context in which she lived and wrote. If you believe that meaning resides in the transaction between the reader and the text, you will place high value on instruction that facilitates meaningful transactions between readers and texts; the process of doing this includes attending to the reader and her background, the text itself, and the social, cultural, and historical context in which the text was written.

Like other scholars (e.g., Beers & Probst, 2013; Kucan & Palincsar, 2013) we advocate a transactional model of reading (as depicted in Figure 3.2) because we believe it captures all the important components—reader, text, and context, including the situation and purpose for reading—needed to foster meaningful disciplinary literacy instruction. Moreover, the notion of the interrelationship between the reader, text, and context is the basis for Reading Anchor Standard 10 in the Common Core.

Component Three: Know Your Students

Teachers need to know their students as people as well as literacy learners. Have you ever picked up a children's book and thought it would be "perfect" for a particular student? Connecting readers to texts is fundamental for engagement and learning. Figure 3.2 represents the complex knowledge you need as a teacher to effectively guide readers' transactions with texts in educative ways. For example, you need to know your students' reading abilities, including background knowledge about words, texts, text structures, genres, and their knowledge and experiences living in the world (Winch, Johnston, March, Ljungdahl, & Holliday, 2011). Students with little knowledge of nonfiction texts, disciplinary vocabulary, and/or disciplinary content knowledge will need intensive and targeted instruction in these areas. You need to understand what interests, motivates, and engages your students (Winch et al., 2011). Further, the more you know about children's lives and world experiences, the more you can build on students' backgrounds as an instructional foundation in your teaching (Brock, 2007; Brock & Raphael, 2005). The fulcrum in Figure 3.2 can move as necessary depending on your children's learning needs and your instructional goals, depicted by the wheels on which the fulcrum rests.

Component Four: Knowledge of Texts and Text Features

Teachers need knowledge of texts and text features. As a teacher, you make countless decisions each minute. Choosing the right texts means drawing on knowledge about the array of available options and aligning the options with your students' needs and interests. It means deciding what support children need as you guide their transactions with texts. As Figure 3.2 illustrates, there are times when you will decide to focus more heavily on "texts" during instruction. This is especially true when using the many different kinds of nonfiction texts needed for disciplinary teaching. Three text features are especially important for disciplinary teaching, including genre, text structures, and graphics and graphic features (Kucan & Palincsar, 2013).

First, genre refers to kinds of texts and their purposes (Derewianka & Jones, 2012). Genres important for disciplinary literacy include nonfiction texts (e.g., a biography of a historical figure), persuasive texts (e.g., a politician's campaign speech), and descriptive texts (e.g., a science text that describes the process of photosynthesis). Second, there are different kinds of informational text structures especially pertinent for disciplinary instruction, including cause/effect, problem/solution, comparison, and chronology. Nonfiction children's books may be designed based on one or more of these text structures. Additionally, short articles in children's magazines or on websites for children (e.g., *National Geographic Kids*, http://kids.national-geographic.com/kids/stories/) are often written using one or more of these text structures. Third, graphics and graphic features are common in texts used for disciplinary instruction, and students need to learn how to interpret them to understand nonfiction texts (Kucan & Palincsar, 2013). Graphics include illustrations, tables, maps, charts, timelines, and the like. Graphic features include titles, headings, and subheadings.

Component Five: Knowledge of Instructional Practices and Assessment

Teachers need to implement effective instructional practices with texts and with assessments that reflect the different types of meaning-making processes that teachers help students to develop and use in disciplinary instruction. In the subsections that follow, we address instructional practices as they relate to disciplinary literacy and then we discuss assessment.

Instructional Practices. Research on reading has much to contribute to our thinking about disciplinary literacy instruction as we look at long-standing effective reading practices. For example, a few of the many research-based reading instructional approaches that can be used in conjunction with, or alongside, disciplinary literacy include guided reading (e.g., Fountas & Pinnell, 2006), the Interactive Strategies Approach (Scanlon, Anderson, & Sweeney, 2010), Book Club (Raphael & McMahon, 1994), reciprocal teaching (Palincsar & Brown, 1984), word study (Bear, Invernizzi, Templeton, & Johnston, 2011), and Reading Recovery (Clay, 1993). Elisabeth, Cassandra, and Mary all used a Book Club instructional framework with its emphasis on connecting reading, writing, and talk as one component of their respective units. Mary and Cassandra used word study as they worked with their students to explore disciplinary vocabulary and concepts.

Although we believe that there are many important reading instructional practices and frameworks to consider relative to disciplinary literacy instruction, we highlight close reading in this subsection because it can be especially useful for reading complex disciplinary texts. Because text complexity and rigor are important topics in the field of reading at present (Beers & Probst, 2013), we say a few words about text complexity and rigor before moving on to discuss close reading.

Text Complexity and Rigor. Since the adoption of the CCSS, much has been said and written about text complexity and rigor (e.g., Fisher, Frey, & Lapp, 2012; Hiebert, 2012). One argument is that students need to read more complex texts because doing so will increase rigor in the classroom (Coleman & Pimentel, 2012). Referring back to Chapter 1 and our discussion of dual commitments (e.g., Florio-Ruane & Raphael, 2004; Raphael, Florio-Ruane, & George, 2001), we agree that students need access to complex age-appropriate text—the first commitment. However, students also need help advancing their reading skills; this happens when you work with them at their instructional levels—the second commitment. When students are asked to read content area materials that are age-appropriate but written above their reading level, teachers need to tailor support to readers based on their unique needs. For some readers, it may be format—figures, charts, graphs. For others, it may involve vocabulary and/or decoding. Scaffolding needs to be geared to whatever it is that makes the text complex to the student who is reading it. It is less about whether students are reading at grade level and more about examining the interaction between what the reader can do independently and what she needs to do to engage fully with the material presented. Ideally, the material will be slightly above the student's reading level; thus, scaffolding helps the student engage with the material in meaningful ways. Sometimes, the text is quite beyond the child's reading level. In this case, scaffolding needs to provide the student with access to the print (e.g., through read-alouds, audio recordings) so she can understand the ideas she is encountering as she reads the text. In all cases, it is important to keep in mind all of the components described, especially the reading context and knowledge of your students.

Close Reading. Beers and Probst (2013) define close reading as bringing "the text and the reader *close* together" in the following manner: "close attention to the text, close attention to the relevant experience, thought, and memory of the reader; close attention to the responses and interpretations of other readers; and close attention to the interactions among those elements" (p. 36). Close reading has typically been the purview of high school and college. However, given the focus on the disciplines in the CCSS, it makes sense to teach close reading at the elementary level when teaching disciplinary literacy. Working with a group of elementary teachers, Fisher and Frey (2012) adapted close reading practices to meet the needs of elementary students.

Fisher and Frey (2012) recommend attending to four issues when implementing close reading at the elementary level. First, pay attention to *who is doing the reading*. The teacher may do read-alouds for young children because they often cannot decode complex disciplinary texts. However, older elementary students typically read the texts independently.

Second, consider the issue of *frontloading*. Frontloading refers to the amount of prereading instruction you provide. How much should you frontload before reading a complex text or asking your students to read a complex text? The teachers who worked with Fisher and Frey (2012) answered this question with, "It depends." They felt that there should not be so much frontloading that it removes the need to actually read the text. Additionally, because close reading focuses heavily on exploring a text in depth, frontloading should keep readers focused on the text rather than focusing on their own experiences too soon.

Third, introduce text-dependent questions that can only be answered as a result of reading a text. Fisher and Frey (2012) introduced six kinds of text-dependent questions that you can use with your students: general understanding questions that focus on the big ideas of a text, key detail questions (questions that answer who, what, when, where, why, and how), questions about vocabulary and text structure, questions about the author's purpose, inferential questions, and intertextual questions that require the reader to look across texts to answer a question.

Fourth, teach your students annotation. Do you recall highlighting your texts in college and making notes in the margins? If so, you likely spent considerable time annotating the texts you read. Annotation refers to making notes for yourself as you read. Although annotation is a common practice for college students, it is not common for elementary students, nor do elementary teachers often have much experience teaching annotation (Fisher & Frey, 2012). Fisher, Frey, and the teachers with whom they worked came up with a series of ideas for teaching annotation to elementary students. They suggest using Wikki Stix for very young children. See the following website for an example of Wikki Stix: http://www.wikkistix.com/what_are_wikkistix.php. Wikki Stix are like strings of clay that stick to books, whiteboards, and so on. Teachers can use them to underline important words, phrases, and sentences so that children can see the underlined print from a distance. Then, as students get older, they can use sticky notes and/or bookmarks to identify major points in a text, exclamation marks for things that surprise them, and question marks for questions or points of confusion they have during their reading.

Assessment: Quality assessments reflect the different types of meaning-making processes teacher use in disciplinary instruction. Assessment of reading instruction should be multifaceted, addressing the different meaning-making processes included in disciplinary literacy instruction. The assessment process informs you as a teacher about two key areas: (1) the effectiveness of your instruction, and (2) students' abilities. Assessment should not be viewed as an event, but rather as an ongoing process of gathering information about what students know (e.g., about the disciplinary content, tools for accessing this content) and what they are able to do (e.g., engage with the disciplinary norms, use tools to gather information). Assessment systems should include a variety of *formative assessments* (to help teachers monitor and guide student learning in progress), *summative assessments* (to help teachers measure student learning after instruction), and other *classroom-based assessments* (to help inform instruction, but not necessarily to evaluate students) (Nitko, 1996).

To measure growth as students are engaged in disciplinary literacy instruction, students should be assessed before, during, and after instruction. Assessments can be informal (e.g., anecdotal records) or formal (e.g., tests, projects), but the purpose of the assessment and the information it will provide should be clear. For example, *before reading*, you can assess the background knowledge of students related to the content, as Elisabeth did with her students studying Sacagawea. It was imperative for her to understand what her students already knew about Sacagawea before engaging in the unit. In this case, students had very little information about the topic, so Elisabeth supplemented with read-alouds of nonfiction texts to build students' background knowledge. In other cases, students may know a lot about a topic or have misinformation on a topic. Assessing knowledge prior to instruction allows you to plan targeted instruction that meets the needs of your students. Other informal assessment tools that can be used prior to reading include K-W-L charts (Ogle, 1986) or concept maps requiring students to organize information about disciplinary content in specific ways.

During reading, you can assess how your students engage with the text and make meaning, including their ability to read in discipline-specific ways (e.g., like a historian or mathematician). For example, Elisabeth knows that historians read texts critically, wondering about the biases and perspectives that the writers have brought to the texts they write (Shanahan & Shanahan, 2008). Consequently, as her students read primary source documents, Elisabeth takes anecdotal records about their reading behaviors, noting whether or not they identify how different words and phrases reveal writers' perspectives and biases. Additionally, as your students are reading and discussing nonfiction disciplinary texts, you may ask them to stop and record or discuss information (e.g., how they interpret timelines, maps, text boxes, and so on as they read). These activities serve dual purposes—they provide information about how students are making sense of what they are reading and also serve as metacognitive instructional strategies.

After reading, you can assess students' overall understanding of a text by asking them to synthesize information, make intertextual connections with other texts across the disciplines, or analyze texts to make their own judgments (Fisher & Frey, 2012). You can also engage students in project-based assessments such as the timelines pertaining to Sacagawea's life that Elisabeth taught her students to create and read. Authentic assessment tasks such as a timeline require students to analyze a great deal of information and represent their understandings (e.g., sequencing, important events, contextual and cultural influences, interrelations across texts, and so forth) through the creation of a multimodal text.

Assessment and Knowledge of Students' Abilities. In addition to explicit reading assessments, you can gather information to increase knowledge about your students (e.g., interests, background information, strengths, challenges, interpersonal skills). Classrooms are becoming increasingly collaborative and, especially in disciplinary study, require students to engage in active inquiry. To ensure that your classroom environment is maximally beneficial for this type of learning, you can explicitly instruct and assess interpersonal and research skills that may not be part of traditional reading assessments. These skills (e.g., creativity, innovation, research, problem solving, communication, and collaboration) directly influence students' abilities to engage in critical thinking across the curriculum and are a part of the elementary technology standards (International Society for Technology in Education, 2007).

DISCIPLINARY LITERACY AND READING

To help you get started on transforming your classroom to include reading as a tool for disciplinary learning, we share examples of classroom reading instruction from Elisabeth's 4th- and Cassandra's 6th-grade classroom, embedded within their conceptual units on remembering Sacagawea and learning about budgets to write persuasive arguments, respectively. Elisabeth uses a conceptual framework focused on remembering Sacagawea to introduce her 4th-graders to: (1) reading and interpreting across multiple sources and (2) using graphics to develop historical understandings. In Cassandra's 6th–grade class, students draw on conceptual knowledge about budgeting and the economy using math content knowledge to: (1) assess claims and weigh evidence, (2) assume a skeptical and questioning stance toward data, and (3) unearth faulty reasoning. Both sets of classroom examples draw on the five key components of disciplinary reading instruction described in Figure 3.2 above.

Examples of Reading History in 4th Grade

So, what does it look like to teach history-specific reading practices in an elementary classroom? Elisabeth draws on research from Bruce VanSledright (2002) to inform her own history teaching. VanSledright, a history teacher educator, spent half a year in a 5th-grade classroom studying how to teach elementary students how historians do the work of history. Drawing on VanSledright's work, Elisabeth understands that general reading comprehension processes, although important, won't suffice as she strives to teach her students to learn to read in discipline-specific ways. Like VanSledright (2002), Elisabeth views the process of "reading" history on a continuum from novice to expert. The overall goal of this kind of history-specific reading is to foster students' historical understanding. At Level 1 of the continuum, VanSledright (2002) argues that when readers use comprehension monitoring to check details, reread, summarize, and/or make initial sense of a source, they are engaging in intratextual (i.e., within-a-text) analysis and reading at the lowest level of expertise. At Level 2, the reader can judge "aspects of a source by indicating whether its various elements make sense and internally cohere" (p. 112). When reading at Level 2, then, the reader is evaluating the text she is reading; this evaluation is still intratextual (i.e., within-a-text). Although Level 2 is more sophisticated than Level 1, according to VanSledright (2002), it still involves general reading practices.

Levels 3 and 4, on the other hand, involve history-specific strategic expertise (VanSledright, 2002). Readers reading at Level 3 acknowledge greater event knowledge, identify the authors in sources and corroborate details across sources, and use growing knowledge from multiple sources to construct an initial interpretation of an event. When reading at Level 3, readers use intertextual analyses because they are working across texts rather than within one text. Reading at Level 4 involves making "intertextual evaluations of the sources' validity, reliability, subtext, and agent intentions as a means of constructing a refined, evidence-based interpretation of an event" (p. 112). Reading at this level involves reading across texts (i.e., intertextually), making critical evaluations of the texts being read. In the section that follows, we provide concrete examples of how Elisabeth began to teach her students to read like historians, attending to several levels of reading on VanSledright's (2002) continuum. Figure 3.3 (adapted from VanSledright, 2002) provides an overview of a continuum of history-specific reading practices. We have highlighted portions of Levels 1, 2, and 3 below with bold because these are the levels that Elisabeth emphasized in her instruction during the unit on remembering Sacagawea.

Figure 3.3. Continuum of History-Specific Reading Practices

GENERAL READING PRACTICES		HISTORY-SPECIFIC READING PRACTICES	
LEVEL 1 (LOWEST LEVEL OF READING EXPERTISE)	LEVEL 2	LEVEL 3	LEVEL 4 (HIGHEST LEVEL OF READING EXPERTISE)
• **Readers use comprehension monitoring to check details, reread, summarize, and/or make initial sense of a source.** • **Intratextual (i.e., within-a-text analysis).**	**The reader is evaluating the text she is reading; this evaluation is still intratextual (i.e., within-a-text).**	• **Readers display a greater understanding of historical events.** • Readers identify the authors in sources and corroborate details across sources. • **Readers use growing knowledge from multiple sources to construct an initial interpretation of an event.** • Readers use intertextual analyses because they are working across texts rather than within one text.	• Reading at Level 4 involves making "intertextual evaluations of the sources' validity, reliability, subtext, and agent intentions as a means of constructing a refined, evidence-based interpretation of an event" (VanSledright, 2002, p. 112). • Reading at this level involves reading across texts (i.e., intertextually), making critical evaluations of the texts being read.

46

Reading and interpreting across multiple sources

Elisabeth's students read the book *Who Was Sacagawea?* (Fradin & Fradin, 2002) as the anchor text for the unit. The students read and listened to many other texts during the overall unit (e.g., Adler, 2003; Rowland, 1983) (Design Principle 4: Range of Resources). For example, one day Elisabeth used a 20-minute read-aloud of an informational book entitled *The Story of Sacagawea, Guide to Lewis and Clark* (Rowland, 1989). This chapter book focuses fairly extensively on Sacagawea's life as a young girl. Elisabeth coordinated read-alouds during the unit with sections of her anchor text so that the read-alouds provided complementary information that helped her students better understand the historical ideas presented in their anchor text. Another read-aloud provided background information about Sacagawea's life. For example, when Sacagawea was 11 years old, Minatare Indians attacked her tribe and kidnapped her. Elisabeth helped the students realize that Sacagawea was about their age when she was kidnapped and taken captive by a different tribe. This example of Elisabeth's reading instruction illustrates how she used multiple resources (i.e., read-alouds in conjunction with her anchor text) to help her students begin to develop a greater understanding of historical events (Design Principle 2: Scaffolding). Notice Elisabeth's instructional practices focus on Level 3, the 1st and 3rd bullets, in Figure 3.3.

By spending time teaching her students to draw on multiple resources, Elisabeth helped the students build historical understandings. She began her unit on remembering Sacagawea by posing the following question to her 29 4th-grade students: "What do you know about Sacagawea, Thomas Jefferson, and Lewis and Clark?" After giving her students a few minutes to reflect silently, she asked them to open their journals and write down everything they knew about Sacagawea, Thomas Jefferson, Meriwether Lewis, and William Clark. Following several minutes of writing time, Elisabeth asked the students to share aloud some of what they had written in their journals. Several students said that they knew that Sacagawea was Native American, but did not know much beyond that. A few students knew that Thomas Jefferson had been president of the United States. No one had heard of Lewis or Clark. Later that afternoon during her prep time, as Elisabeth read the students' journal entries for the day, Vanessa's writing captured what most of the students knew about the four historical figures. Vanessa wrote, "I don't know nothing."

In contrast, by the end of the unit, Vanessa wrote two single-spaced pages explaining the context surrounding Sacagawea's life and why we should remember her. Among other ideas, Vanessa wrote (her temporary spellings reproduced here): "Sacagawea is a gret women. She's the resen we know now what is in the west and she was included in Clark's jorle [journal]." Vanessa's post-assessment was representative of the increased knowledge of her classmates as well. Every child in class wrote one to two single-spaced pages explaining what she or he learned about Sacagawea and why it is important to remember her. Elisabeth's work developing her students' conceptual understanding of Sacagawea's life and experiences illustrates how she addressed the third component of disciplinary reading instruction— attending carefully to her students as individuals and literacy learners and designing her instructional practices to meet their instructional needs. She also addressed the fifth component of disciplinary reading instruction— using authentic summative assessment practices to ascertain what her students learned across the unit.

Using graphics to develop historical understandings

Elisabeth taught her students about timelines and maps to help them learn to differentiate between what is and what is not historically significant and to develop a sense of chronology (Design Principle 4: Range of Resources). Building a timeline provides a concrete way to help students learn to read critically by differentiating between what is and is not historically significant. There are two important components for establishing historical significance (Seixas, 1993). First, students need to understand that not everything in history is important or significant, reinforcing the notion that history is constructed through the research and interpretation of historians (Levstik & Barton, 2010; Seixas, 1993). Second, students need to understand that what counts as significant may differ across time and cultures. For example, what is historically significant to the descendants of White explorers may differ from what is historically significant to Native Americans, and different Native American groups will also assign different levels of significance to different events.

Creating and reading timelines

Elisabeth's students collaborated in pairs to create timelines. Timelines are typical of nonfiction text that encourages a conceptual map of a time period, and teaching timelines is a required component of the social studies curriculum. Based on the information that students had already learned, as well as new information they were continuing to learn, the pairs begin to list what they thought were the most significant events of Sacagawea's life. Many students included information from the first chapter, including 1789/1790, when Sacagawea was born; 1800, when she was kidnapped; and then, from information provided in their focus biography, some of them inferred that Sacagawea would have been 15 in 1804 when Charbonneau took her to begin the Lewis and Clark expedition. Also, many timelines included the year 2000, when the U.S. government issued the Sacagawea coin. This activity addresses the first aspect of historical significance as the students critically evaluate what is significant and what is not, choosing to include only certain information. Elisabeth reminded the students that one criterion for determining significance was to consider the key unit question: Why do we remember Sacagawea? (Design Principle 3: Key Inquiry Questions).

The opportunity to work in pairs and compare timelines addresses the second aspect of historical significance (i.e., what counts as significant may differ across time, settings, and cultures). In this concrete experience, students compared how—based on their interpretation of texts, their prior knowledge, and their sociocultural positions—they differed in their interpretation (representing their own beliefs and biases) of the significance/triviality of certain events (Design Principle 1: Authentic Social & Cultural Practices). This occurred as the pairs negotiated what should go on their timeline and again when they compared their timelines. Elisabeth also asked the students to include the current year on the timeline so they could develop a sense of "close to now" versus "long ago" (Levstik & Barton, 2010), relative to the important events they were studying. Using equivalent increments of every 10 years from 1770 to the present, students also create a visual cue as to how some significant events were clustered in a relatively short period of time and how there were long passages of time between other events. Because the students had created their own timelines, they developed a sense of how timelines "work." Consequently, when students encountered timelines in other nonfiction texts, they were better able to read and interpret them.

Reading maps

In addition to teaching the students about timelines as they read their focus unit text, Elisabeth also addressed the five themes of geography (i.e., location, place, regions, movement, human-environment interactions) as they related to the unit. Along with other types of nonfiction texts, maps can be an engaging way for students to read for information and pay attention to text features critical to understanding content. For example, to examine the theme of *place*, each child received a historical map of the United States with political boundaries (e.g., states and territories) of the time of Lewis and Clark's expedition and major natural landmarks such as the Snake River. The students used the maps as they progressed through the story. Elisabeth emphasized that the boundaries of current states such as Montana, Idaho, Washington, Oregon, and North Dakota are not on the map because they were not states then. But the physical places such as the Bitterroot and Rocky Mountains *are* on the map. Elisabeth uses this distinction between the human characteristics of a place (i.e., the human-constructed elements of political boundaries, towns) and the physical characteristics of a place (i.e., mountains, rivers) to reinforce the geography theme of place. As students discussed new places on their map throughout the unit, they determined whether the maps displayed human or physical characteristics (Design Principle 2: Scaffolding).

In labeling and discussing the Missouri River on their maps, Elisabeth helped students understand why expedition leaders chose to travel by river, a concept pertaining to an Illinois social science standard on transportation. Without roads or railroads, lakes and rivers were the best way to travel, resulting in the development of early settlements around bodies of water. To reinforce this transportation-related pattern of human settlement, Elisabeth showed a video about transportation and displayed a historical map of colonial America detailing human settlements (Design Principle 4: Range of Resources). The students had already studied colonial America and were able to recall the importance of individual cities such as New York (on the Hudson River) and Philadelphia (on the Delaware River), as well as the location of other cities on the Atlantic coast in the development of the United States.

To create a current and locally relevant connection to the students, Elisabeth also shared a map of Chicago, asking students to apply what they know about Chicago's history. In reading the map, she reinforced their new understanding of the cultural universal of transportation (Brophy & Alleman, 2006), and the importance of bodies of water in where people settle to answer the question: How might the existence of Lake Michigan and the Chicago River (physical characteristics) make the development of a settlement (human characteristic) likely?

Elisabeth taught her students to develop and interpret timelines and maps to explore geography themes, historical understandings, and historical significance, illustrating instruction focused on Levels 1 and 3 (the 1st and 3rd bullets) of Figure 3.3. That is, she helped her students make initial sense of various texts and sources and used multiple sources such as informational texts (including maps and timelines) to help them build knowledge of, and interpret, historical events pertaining to Sacagawea's life (Design Principle

2: Scaffolding). Additionally, Elisabeth's instruction with maps and time-lines enacted the fourth component of effective disciplinary reading instruction—teaching students to read and interpret texts and text features.

Examples of Reading Mathematically in 6th Grade

Like Elisabeth, Cassandra uses her knowledge of her students, the reading process, content, and literacy and discipline-related processes to make important instructional decisions. Also like Elisabeth, Cassandra understands that reading in mathematics differs from reading in other content areas (Design Principle 1: Social Cultural Contexts). Because Cassandra believes that her students should learn to use math in meaningful ways for real-world purposes, her instruction focuses on quantitative literacy rather than solely on traditional mathematics (Miller, 2010; Wiest, Higgins, & Frost, 2007).

Research on quantitative literacy provides background for how Cassandra taught her students to read mathematically. Quantitative literacy does involve traditional mathematics, such as computational skills and number sense; however, quantitative literacy also involves "the ability to make reasoned decisions using general world knowledge and fundamental mathematics in authentic, everyday circumstances" (Wiest et al., 2007, p. 48). Cassandra wanted her students to successfully *do* and *use* traditional mathematics as they made decisions about the quality of data to use in their letters to Governor Sandoval. Hence, she developed the unit on budgeting to use math in meaningful ways in real-world contexts.

Quantitative literate reading requires the ability to (1) assess claims and weigh evidence, (2) assume a skeptical and questioning stance toward data, and (3) unearth faulty reasoning. Additionally, quantitative literate reading requires facility with essential mathematical knowledge and skills, including facility with numbers, statistical and probabilistic knowledge and reasoning—including data representation and interpretation in graphic and other forms, reasoning and problem-solving skills, a basic command of geometry, measurement, proportional reasoning, algebra, and the ability to use technological tools such as calculators and computers (Wiest et al., 2007). Throughout her unit, Cassandra used a variety of different kinds of texts to teach her students to read in quantitatively literate ways, including word problems, read-alouds of picture books such as *How Much Is a Million?* (Schwartz & Kellogg, 1994) and *The True Story of the Three Little Pigs* (Schieszka, 1989), newspaper articles from the Internet, and so forth. In the examples that follow, we illustrate how Cassandra used word problems to teach her students to read in quantitatively literate ways.

We focus on word problems for three reasons (Wiest, 2003). First, word problems are one of the most typical kinds of math texts that students read. Second, word problems are some of the most difficult reading that students encounter. Third, Cassandra knew that the students would be doing Internet research to include data/evidence in their letters to Governor Sandoval. She reasoned that the kinds of number-related issues the students would encounter as they sought sources for their letters would be represented in word problems similar to the ones we present here.

Assessing claims and weighing evidence

Cassandra used word problems with her students to help them use their knowledge of math to assess claims and weigh evidence. She wrote the following word problem on the write board and modeled how to read and reread it closely:

> Is driving 10 miles over the speed limit equally remiss in both a 25 mile-per-hour (mph) and a 65 mph zone?

The students talked with a partner to discuss the statement, and then shared their ideas with the whole class.

Jorge and Esteban explained that just looking at the absolute number of 10 miles over the speed limit does not tell the whole story mathematically. The proportion of difference between 25 and 35 is much higher than the proportion of difference between 65 and 75.

Araceli and Marc reasoned that the 25 mph zone was probably in a neighborhood because that is the typical speed limit for residential areas. Consequently, driving 10 miles over the speed limit could increase the risk of hitting a child, an animal, or a bicyclist on a neighborhood street. Typically, the speed limit on a freeway or highway is 65 mph. Although driving faster on a freeway could increase the risk of an accident, it is far less likely that a motorist would hit a child, animal, or bicyclist on a freeway or highway.

Thus, in this example, students used mathematical knowledge of proportions to analyze and interpret written data. Cassandra pointed out that students might encounter examples like this as they sought evidence from various Internet sources to include in the letters they would be writing to Governor Sandoval. She reminded students that they would need to draw on what they know about mathematics to analyze and interpret any data they considered using in their letters.

Assuming a skeptical and questioning attitude toward data.

Cassandra wrote the word *burglary* on the whiteboard and asked the students what the word meant. Once the class discussed its meaning, she put the following word problem on the document camera and asked the students to read it:

> Two Mills, Pennsylvania, had two bikes stolen in the past year. Does this town have a low or high burglary rate? Does it seem to be a safe place to live or visit?

Following paired discussion, students shared their ideas. For example, Julio and Adrianna said that they wouldn't want to live in or visit the town because it seemed dangerous. Brisa and Juan, on the other hand, said that it depended on the size of the town. If only four bikes were in the town and two of them were stolen, that would be a 50% burglary rate. However, if the town had 1,000 bikes and two of them were stolen, it would only be a burglary rate of .2% (i.e., two-tenths of 1%). Although the class agreed that any burglaries at all would be bad, the population of a town in relation to stolen bikes must be taken into account when answering the questions the teacher posed.

As another example, Cassandra wrote the following statement on the whiteboard and asked the students to read, reread, and then interpret it: "Does an average height of 5'9" seem like an accurate average height for a group of people?" Again, after discussing the question in dyads first and then in the whole group, the class decided that it would need to know if the group of people was composed of professional basketball players (in which 5'9" would be too short), horse-racing jockeys (in which case 5'9" would be too tall), elementary students (in which case 5'9" would be too tall), and so forth.

Unearthing faulty reasoning

Cassandra also taught her students to beware of faulty reasoning as they were reading from various Internet sources to include data in their letters to Governor Sandoval. For example, she asked her students to read the following brief excerpt of text to see if they could discern the faulty reasoning:

> More people drown swimming in warm than in cold bodies of ocean water. Therefore, warm water is more likely to cause drowning, so it is more dangerous to swim in warm water.

Reading and rereading the text excerpt aloud, Cassandra modeled a think-aloud as she sorted out what she would need to know to determine the validity of the statement. Cassandra reasoned that first it would be wise to see how many people actually swim in warm bodies of water as compared to cold bodies of water. Then, she asked the students to do Internet research to find the answer to her question. Collaborating with a partner, Raul and Jorge used Internet research to determine where most people actually swim. We explain more about how Cassandra taught her students to do Internet research in Chapter 4. Once the students learned that very few people swim in cold bodies of water, Tashina and Chris determined that the faulty reasoning was that people typically only swim in warm water; consequently, because there are many, many more people swimming in warm water, it makes sense that there would be more drowning accidents in warm water.

Cassandra shared the following additional text excerpt with her students: "People have more automobile accidents closer to home. Therefore, driving near home can cause car accidents and is thus more dangerous." This time, Cassandra asked the students to read and reread the text with a partner striving to get very clear about what the text excerpt meant. Again, the students did Internet research to find out where most driving occurs. Their research revealed that most driving occurs within 30 miles of a person's home. Consequently, Clarence and Eliot argued the faulty reasoning is that driving near home *causes* accidents. Since most driving occurs near home, it makes sense that most accidents would occur closer to home because a higher percentage of people drive near their homes. Clarence and Eliot also reasoned that it is important to always wear seatbelts in the car—even when riding in the car for short distances!

As Cassandra used instructional examples with her students such as the ones we have presented here, she addressed two key components of disciplinary reading instruction described earlier: the reading context and texts and text features. First, the context of mathematical reading requires careful reading and rereading of words and numbers as well as attention to the interrelationships between the two (Shanahan & Shanahan, 2008). Cassandra provided expert scaffolding to her students as she taught them to read mathematically. Second, because students often have little meaningful exposure to story problems, they may have difficulty understanding and interpreting them. Consequently, in order to learn to understand story problems, students need more exposure to this unique text structure.

EXAMINING CLASSROOM READING
ACROSS DISCIPLINES

As these examples show, reading serves different purposes and functions in different disciplines. However, there are several features pertaining to reading that matter across the disciplines, too. We end this chapter by bringing together the key reading frameworks tied to examples from the classrooms. Think about how you might incorporate these ideas into your own teaching.

1. Comprehension occurs in the transaction between readers and texts. What the reader brings to the text, the nature of the text itself, and the teacher's role in scaffolding the reading process all shape the transaction that occurs between the reader and the text. Current issues pertaining to reading instruction (e.g., close reading, rigor and text complexity, and the use of text-dependent questions) should all be considered through the lens of reading as a transaction between readers and texts. Moreover, there are many, many research-based instructional approaches and frameworks for reading instruction that should remain in use with the adoption of the CCSS.

2. Teachers must know their children as people and literacy learners. For example, Cassandra could not provide effective instruction in her unit on budgeting if she had not known that her students knew very little about budgets and budgeting prior to the unit. Also, as she used texts during her unit, she realized that her students needed to read texts written at their instructional reading levels, but they need to be exposed to ideas that represent disciplinary content appropriate for their grade levels.

3. Teachers must have knowledge of texts, text structures, and instructional practices with texts. For example, Elisabeth understands that texts used for history instruction are written in ways that are unique to history. Thus, she was able to teach her students to attend to specific text features as they read their informational texts. Also, Cassandra spent considerable time teaching her students to read mathematically by being critical consumers of the texts they read.

4. Teachers must have knowledge of social/cultural/historical contexts. Both Elisabeth and Cassandra realize that students need to learn to read different kinds of texts pertinent to different disciplines in different ways.

To read disciplinary texts effectively in a variety of contexts, students must become facile with and wisely use conventional print, websites, etc.

   5. Assessments have to reflect the different types of meaning-making processes teachers use in instruction. Assessment should be a continuous process of data gathering that provides teachers with information to guide instruction before, during, and after reading. Assessment systems should include multiple data sources that evaluate students' reading abilities, as well as interpersonal and research skills.

CHAPTER 4

Writing Within and Across Texts

Virginia Goatley, David Crowther, Julie Pennington,
Cynthia Brock, Taffy Raphael, and Catherine Weber

Writing should be full of inquiry, engagement, and purpose. When writing daily, students think about audience and purpose, and the form to use as they determine what and how to write. In this chapter, we explore writing in the disciplines (e.g., informational, observations), primary sources (e.g., interviews), and digital texts (e.g., gathering evidence on the Internet). Using writing in the disciplines is consistent with good practice in writing and aligns with Common Core writing standards that have high expectations for stronger connections to disciplinary learning. This chapter describes how to use writing as a way to teach students the conceptual aspects of the disciplines. To help you create effective writing instruction in your classroom, we provide examples of how students write, drawing on Mary's and Cassandra's use of writing to teach scientific and mathematical concepts. Figure 4.1 describes writing instruction in terms of the Core Design Principles described in Chapter 1.

WHAT MATTERS
ABOUT WRITING INSTRUCTION

Writing can be powerful! Especially when, consistent with Design Principle 1, writing engages students in authentic social and cultural practices. Think about real-world uses for writing, how such writing varies by purpose and intent, and implications for instruction. In this chapter, we present three components of a coherent writing instructional framework: (1) student experiences with disciplinary writing and written texts, (2) resources to meet writing purposes, and (3) assessment for purposeful writing.

Figure 4.1. Core Design Principles in Writing

Design Principle	Example
1. Authentic Social and Cultural Practices	Connect writing to everyday conceptual tasks of the discipline (e.g., observation note-taking, writing persuasive letters). Understand writing as a tool to persuade.
2. Optimal Learning Model	Model and assist students to learn new concepts, such as Internet research.
3. Key Inquiry Questions	Develop an understanding of inquiry to drive questioning and research to learn new concepts (e.g., environment, budgets).
4. Composing Requires a Range of Resources	Teach students to draw on resources such as read-aloud content, artifacts, Internet research, and interviews with experts in their writing.
5. Authentic Assessments Reflect Meaning-Making Process	Assess students by having them write a class book for another grade level or a persuasive letter for a government official.

Component One: Experiences with Disciplinary Writing

Students need experiences with disciplinary writing and written texts used in the disciplines. Students can gain experiences with disciplinary writing and written texts used in the disciplines if we provide (1) experiences reading and writing a wide variety of texts used in the disciplines, and (2) authentic instructional experiences pertaining to the disciplines.

Provide experiences with a wide variety of disciplinary texts

Think about the last time you wrote a letter to inform parents of your classroom activities or their students' progress, an email to persuade your senator, or a complaint to a service provider. Did you write each with the same intent, format, or voice? Did you draw on relevant evidence to support your ideas? Chances are, you were quite intent on making sure that your word choices, tone, and length helped you make the point you needed to make for that particular audience.

In a similar way, students need experience reading and writing texts (e.g., speeches, interviews, notes, blogs) relevant to the disciplines. As shown in Figure 2.1, students should have writing experiences associated with informational texts, digital media, and primary sources, in addition to the more commonly used fiction. For example, writing instruction can emphasize how to share an opinion or write a persuasive argument in favor of an idea, both of which might be quite engaging to students. Disciplinary goals for writing help students reenvision the audience and purpose for writing, much like professionals in various careers.

It is helpful to keep a few key research studies in mind as you plan writing instruction. Given what we know about the limited number of informational texts students read in elementary school (Duke, 2000; Jeong, Gaffney, & Choi, 2010; Yopp & Yopp, 2012), it follows logically that writing informational and persuasive texts is also limited (Kamberelis, 1998). Even when teachers do use informational text for read-alouds in the classroom, Yopp and Yopp (2012) found that the majority was related to science content, rather than the other disciplines. Further, within science-related genres written for children, Pappas (2006) suggests that teachers need to carefully consider which books are most appropriate for science instruction in terms of the linguistic registers of the discipline. What do these studies tell us? We need to greatly expand the amount of time and the type of text that students spend listening to, reading, and writing related to the disciplines.

Just think for a moment about how much time your students spent with inquiry by reading and writing connected texts during your most recent teaching day. How many texts connected to a genre other than fiction? These questions are an obvious first step to increase disciplinary concepts and vocabulary that students encounter on a daily basis. But there are many other steps to take beyond increasing time. If you focus on inquiry, students will likely find reading and writing a variety of genres to be more engaging—you might even need to figure out new writing ideas to help them find answers to their content-related questions. For example, Redford (2011) strongly encourages us to nurture students' mathematical curiosity by valuing the questions that students ask. Burton and Mims (2012) focused on inquiry when they asked 1st-graders, "How do you measure a puddle?" The 1st-graders wrote possible strategies for how they might use tools (e.g., ruler, measuring cup) to solve this problem.

With advances in technology, we have access to a greater variety and number of texts related to the disciplines (e.g., databases, historical artifacts, graphic organizers). For example, Potter (2009) describes how to use the National Archives website with numerous historical documents (http://

go.fold3.com/nara/). While there has traditionally been a dearth of informational texts written for children, publishers have increased production in the last decade (Cooperative Children's Book Center, 2013). This strongly positions us to use these tools as a way to better support students in using resources to write within particular disciplines (Principle 4).

Provide authentic instructional experiences
pertaining to the disciplines

Research studies connecting science education to writing informational texts send a clear message about the importance of authenticity for informing instructional plans for writing (Principle 1). Purcell-Gates, Duke, and Martineau (2007) found 2nd- and 3rd-graders "involved in *authentic* literacy events with informational and procedural texts in science is impressively related to their degree of growth in their abilities to both comprehend and produce such texts" (p. 41). Similarly, in her study with 1st-graders, Wollman-Bonilla (2000) suggests that students need to "do science," where they learn to write like a scientist. This includes learning the genres and conventions of how scientists write, but also the ability to question and rework texts as their knowledge grows. If you are looking for a helpful book with specific details on teaching genre, see Duke, Caughlan, Juzwik, and Martin (2012). They offer research-based instructional ideas about how to teach genre with a focus on the purpose for reading and writing. They separate narrative, procedural, informational, dramatic, and persuasive genres as five distinct ways of considering texts.

Keep in mind, even young students can write documents connected to real-world applications. Rebecca Powell (a teacher educator) and Nancy Davidson (a classroom teacher) collaborated on a literacy project with urban kindergarten students (Powell & Davidson, 2005). The young students visited a donut shop, reading and recording many ideas to use subsequently as they built and opened their own Donut House in their classroom. In the process, the kindergartners wrote a wide range of documents, including invitations, stock certificates, building permits, letters, lists, loan applications, and so forth. The authors contrasted school literacy with literacy situated in genuine social practices. They provided descriptive details of how the kindergartners engaged in numerous writing events for real audiences while connecting with various members of the community. What these students accomplished is a valuable reminder of the need to keep high expectations for what young children can write when given highly engaging opportunities with real reasons for exploring ideas.

Component Two: Resources for Writing Purposes

Students need to learn to use a range of resources to gather information, compose arguments, support claims, and address other goals for writing texts. Students can learn to use a range of resources if we (1) show them resources and model their use, (2) use high-quality mentor texts with them, and (3) teach children how to be critical consumers of the texts they use in their own writing.

Show and model the use of resources

If we increase writing connected to the disciplines, such as informational and persuasive writing, what supports do teachers need to provide that differ from those used for story writing? Not surprisingly, it's important to show examples of expository text structures, model how to use and synthesize across multiple sources, and discuss plagiarism concerns. Within disciplines such as history and biology, students need to learn how to draw on information from multiple sources, use evidence to support their claims, and consider the writing structure in terms of what the audience expects.

Use high-quality mentor texts

Just as they do for story writing, mentor or anchor texts play a pivotal role in writing instruction, showing a range of how authors write and how writing structures shift and change depending on purpose (Routman, 2004; Wood Ray, 1999). Mentor texts are sometimes books that are familiar to students, allowing teachers the opportunity to encourage a focus on the written text and the word choices instead of comprehension.

Alternatively, mentor texts that are new to students help them encounter and consider purposes for writing they might not notice on their own. For example, read and analyze a text such as *My Denali: Exploring Alaska's Favorite National Park* (Corral & Corral, 1995) or *Two in the Wilderness* (Weber, 2005). A mother and daughter team contributed to each book, in which the text structures display both autobiographical text and a range of text features for informational purposes (e.g., text box, photograph, highlighted vocabulary).

As illustrated in Figure 4.2, your students could examine how authors present scientific and cultural contextual information both in a narrative and informational format. Figure 4.2 shows how the authors used four different formats for presenting information, with each one contributing a unique

Figure 4.2. Excerpt from Two in the Wilderness

The birch trees that grew in the burned spaces are now old and dying. Balsam and spruce are moving in and will soon return this forest to its old appearance.

By late afternoon, we are pitching our tent beside Indian Pass Brook. Marcy assembles the long poles while I push the tent stakes into the soft dirt. Together, we feed the poles through the tent sleeves and raise the roof. There is just enough room inside for two.

I start our little one-burner gas stove and heat some ravioli and baked beans. It's not fancy food, but it smells delicious.

Marcy takes charge of getting water. She pumps it through a filter because the brook water is not safe to drink untreated. It might contain harmful bacteria that would make us terribly ill.

Surprisingly, Marcy has no trouble with the pump. And I have no problem with the stove. I guess we are both realizing we are fast learners and we make a good team.

After dinner, I sit in the tent and listen to the mosquitoes buzz around the screening. I cannot sleep in the strange surroundings. I also worry about the steep trail that lies ahead, and about the impending rainy days. We are warm and snug tonight, but what about the next week? Rain is predicted for every day.

▶ *Filtering water. Marcy soaks her feet as she pumps water from the stream through a filter and into a water bottle.*

Marcy's Journal
Wednesday, July 30
I suppose this trip is not as boring as I thought. First, Carl Heilman, our photographer, is a fun guy. He bushwhacked over rocks and climbed along high ledges with us. Also, sometimes he makes us walk in slow motion. Other times, he pops up in front of me and takes a picture without warning.

The other excitement today was that I burned my hand. Yeah, the baked beans tipped off the stove, and I dived for the pot. Mom stuck my hand in the cold brook. Then she bandaged it and it felt better.

Concerning our camp: The lean-to was full. So we put our tent in a large, grassy clearing. It is close to the brook and waterfall (Rocky Falls). The gurgling water is very loud.

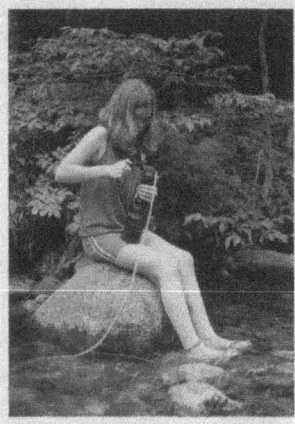

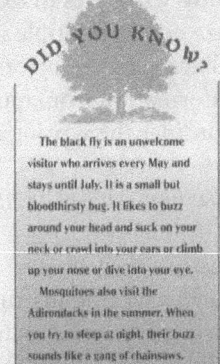

DID YOU KNOW?

The black fly is an unwelcome visitor who arrives every May and stays until July. It is a small but bloodthirsty bug. It likes to buzz around your head and suck on your neck or crawl into your ears or climb up your nose or dive into your eye. Mosquitoes also visit the Adirondacks in the summer. When you try to sleep at night, their buzz sounds like a gang of chainsaws.

perspective on the experiences of visiting the Adirondack Mountains. This example helps students start to distinguish how writing to convey facts, ideas, and perspectives differs from typical story writing.

There are many resources to help you select mentor or anchor texts. You might already be familiar with literature articles in professional journals such as *Language Arts*, *The Reading Teacher*, *Teaching Children Mathematics*, and *The Horn Book*. The professional organizations for discipline-related journals also publish recommended book lists. For example, the National Council for the Social Studies (NCSS, 2013) publishes a list of *Notable Tradebooks for Young People* each year (see http://www.socialstudies.org/resources/notable). Similarly, the National Science Teachers Association (NSTA, 2013) compiles an annual *Outstanding Science Tradebooks for Students K–12* (see http://www.nsta .org/publications/ostb/).

Teach children to be critical consumers of texts

Using sources to support arguments is a complex process for young learners. With more advanced technology options, such as Wikipedia, YouTube, and Facebook, students need to become critical consumers of the websites and social media options around them. Figure 4.3 provides an outline containing six dimensions for evaluating websites from Zhang and colleagues' (2011) WWWDOT project. With the ease of accessibility, we must help students learn to avoid plagiarism, use direct quotes, and provide appropriate attribution for the ideas of other people. The to-do list for the future helps the student stay organized by recording questions, noting links to additional websites, and other information about the topic.

It is amazing how much even young students have already learned about finding information on the Internet. Helping students become critical consumers of what they read is essential to the sciences and history. As the Internet increases students' ability to access primary sources (e.g., ancestry. com) and because such sources are easily manipulated with software (e.g., editing photographs), we need to be especially concerned with helping students learn to carefully use those sources in their own writing.

Component Three: Assessment for Purposeful Writing

Assessments need to reflect the different types of composing processes students will use in real-world settings. Assessments will reflect the different types of composing processes students use in real-world settings if teachers do

Figure 4.3. Criteria for Evaluating Websites

1. Who wrote this and what credentials do they have?
2. Why was it written?
3. When was it written?
4. Does it help meet my needs?
5. Organization of the site?
6. To-do list for the future.

Source: Zhang, Duke, & Jimenez, 2011, p. 152.

the following: (1) Use assessments to understand how students are using the writing process to create a text, (2) ensure that assessments are ongoing and capture different stages of the development, and (3) engage students in authentic assessments that provide information about disciplinary learning and writing in tandem. Explicit instruction should be provided and assessments given in two key areas of writing: (1) process (the stages of writing an author goes through to create a text), and (2) product and craft (how the author accomplishes her purpose) (see Hoyt & Boswell, 2012; Tompkins, 2011).

Use assessments to understand student engagement in writing

When your students are writing, what are the best ways you can learn about their progress? How do you use their writing to inform your instructional decisions? Too often, the emphasis is placed on completed texts, which tells teachers very little about students' strengths and challenges related to writing. Tompkins suggests that the writing process is "a way of looking at writing instruction in which the emphasis is shifted away from finished products to what students think and do as they write" (p. 6).

The writing process is most often taught to students as a formulaic sequence of events that a writer uses to generate a text. However, the process varies considerably depending on the type of text the author is creating, the author's purpose, the audience, and so forth. It is not a lockstep process, but rather an iterative cycle of planning, drafting, revising, and editing. Teachers need to teach students about the variability of the process and how to apply the writing process in different ways across the disciplines.

For example, in this chapter you will read about Cassandra's unit on budgeting in which students gathered information and wrote a persuasive letter to influence policy. Although the letter was the final product, Cassandra focused her assessment on the process students used to write the letter. She wanted to measure students' progress as writers and as disciplinary experts (e.g., math, economics, civics). She gathered information about students' growing understanding of budgets, analysis of resources, and persuasive writing for a specific audience.

Ongoing assessment to capture writing development

Writing should be assessed at every stage (prewriting, drafting, revising, editing, and publishing) of the writing process to inform teachers about students' instructional needs. For example, at the *prewriting* stage, teachers may assess students' abilities to research a topic, organize information, and select an appropriate genre to effectively communicate with a particular audience for a particular purpose. At the *drafting* stage, teachers can assess students' abilities to engage a reader, communicate information, and organize a text coherently. For science, math, and history texts, this might include supporting details and aids (e.g., graphs, text boxes).

During *revising*, assessment may focus on students' abilities to engage in constructive critiques with peers, self-assessment, and making substantive changes to texts. At the *editing* stage, teachers can assess students' ability to proofread and polish their writing. In the final *publication* stage, assessment should focus on both the finished product, using rubrics such as 6+1 traits (Culham, 2003) and others (see Routman, 2004) and students' abilities to share their writing appropriately with the intended audience. Assessing students at each stage of the process provides teachers with the important information they need to plan targeted instruction that develops students as researchers and writers across the disciplines.

For example, you will read about Mary's 2nd-grade students who created books for kindergartners. The completed text was not the only assessment she used to measure students' progress. Throughout the unit, she assessed students' writing and disciplinary learning through the use of science observation notebooks, lists of topics and graphic organizers for prewriting, drafts of informational texts, and collaborative peer revising and editing.

Assessments on disciplinary learning and writing

Teachers need to assess students using a wide range of written products that reflect real-world demands and the types of writing that disciplinary experts use. Although many teachers teach students to write using the writing process and may introduce students to a range of genres, they may not teach students the relationship between the two. That is, the purposes and intended audiences influence writers' decisions about the types of texts they create. If these are not made explicit, it can be difficult for students to make connections between the writing classroom and real-world contexts in which they apply writing.

Furthermore, there is often little instruction on the various types of texts within broad categories of writing. For example, many schools teach writing in the following broad categories: (1) narrative, (2) expository, (3) poetry, and (4) persuasive. Common assessments for these various types of writing include prompts and expectations for formulaic responses, particularly with expository texts in the disciplines. This does not address the plethora of texts students encounter in their daily lives.

Romano (2000) provides teachers an alternative way of assessing students' writing and disciplinary learning simultaneously. Through the use of multigenre writing, students have an opportunity to research topics of interest and present information through various texts, rather than the traditional research paper (e.g., five-paragraph essay). Students learn how to compose many different texts from more traditional (e.g., biographies, speeches, journal entries) to more creative texts (e.g., schedules, budgets, contracts, family trees, observational notes, obituaries). Each piece of text "(u)tilizes a different genre, reveals one facet of the topic, and makes its own point. Conventional devices do not connect the pieces in a multigenre paper, nor are the pieces always in chronological order. The paper is instead a collage of writing and artistic expression with an overarching theme that engulfs and informs the reader" (Allen, 2001, p. 2).

For example, you will read about Mary's unit focused on the environment in which students explored the topic and engaged in a variety of writing activities (e.g., observational notes, science notes about texts they read, graphs, and so on) to present new information they learned. Students did not write the typical research project, but the teacher was able to assess their knowledge about writing and the disciplines.

Students are able to represent disciplinary learning through creative outlets using multigenre writing assessments, which provide teachers with a great deal of information about students' abilities to research a topic, analyze and synthesize information, write for different purposes and audiences, and explore a multitude of authentic texts. This is an effective way to support students as they learn to use writing as a tool for disciplinary learning.

DISCIPLINARY LITERACY AND CLASSROOM WRITING

To help you start transforming your classroom to include writing as a tool for disciplinary learning, we share examples of classroom writing from Mary's 2nd- and Cassandra's 6th-grade classroom, embedded within their themes on caring for the environment and learning about budgets to write persuasive arguments, respectively. The goal is for students to learn that writing involves a range of possibilities such as interviews, observations, note-taking, and persuasion. We start by broadening students' awareness of writing purposes and then support them as they try new ways to write. Mary uses a conceptual framework, the Taking Care of the Environment unit, to introduce her 2nd-graders to (1) taking observational notes, (2) recording ideas and questions, and (3) writing informational text for a kindergarten audience. In Cassandra's 6th grade, students draw on conceptual knowledge about budgeting and the economy using math content knowledge to learn to be critical consumers of text and to write a persuasive letter to a government official. Each of the following examples illustrates three key ideas of disciplinary literacy instruction: (1) Writing is a tool for understanding disciplinary concepts, (2) students need to learn to use a range of resources when writing informational texts, and (3) assessments have to reflect composing processes for real-world settings.

Examples of Science Writing in 2nd Grade

In her 2nd-grade classroom, Mary draws on the five design principles to implement her unit. Her students regularly engaged in writing for many purposes and audiences (Principle 1) and drew on a range of resources to do so (Principle 4). Within the science unit on Taking Care of the Environment, she supported her students in writing informational text (Principle 2), with an authentic goal of creating and sharing a class book with kindergarten reading buddies (Principle 5). During the unit, Mary used children's books representing a range of genres to introduce vocabulary and concepts about the environment, including *On Our Way Home* (Braun, 2009), *Stellaluna* (Cannon, 1993), *I Took a Walk* (Cole, 1998), *The Three Questions* (Muth, 2002), *What If?* (Seeger, 2010), and *Your Environment* (Williams, 1998). She created lessons where students made observations, recorded notes in their science observation books, read additional texts, discussed observations in small groups and pairs, and engaged in whole-group conversations while recording important ideas on flip charts. After observation and discussion, she helped her students review and synthesize ideas across texts. These activities served as both instructional strategies and assessment tools. They provide information to teachers about students' growing knowledge of disciplinary concepts and writing abilities. The following three examples provide a glimpse into the students' daily writing throughout the unit.

Taking observational notes

Students learned to use writing as a tool for understanding concepts employed by disciplinary experts. Recording observational notes is often a daily literacy event for scientists and historians because they need to maintain accurate records of what they've observed and discovered. You might remember lab notebooks from high school science, where you documented information from scientific fieldwork (Weiss-Magasic, 2012). The same writing tool helps students engage in scientific inquiry and remember what they observed. Mary was able to use the observational notes as an authentic assessment of her students' developing knowledge of environmental science. Figure 4.4 shows Robert's notes while he was observing and touching various objects in a mini-environment bowl to determine if they were biotic (living) or abiotic (nonliving) things (see the picture of this activity in Chapter 2).

While Mary pulled together the artifacts for this particular observational activity, there were other options, too. Field trips to events or institutions closely aligned with a conceptual theme offered many opportunities for observation. Gomez (2010) shares how to use field trips as an inquiry tool. If your school eliminated field trips because of budget cuts, Risinger (2010) offers ideas about online field trips and tours in the social studies disciplines.

Recording ideas

Have you ever had a great idea or powerful thought, then were unable to recall it later? Tools used for recording ideas meet authentic purposes for engaging in meaningful disciplinary learning. Second-grader Cole routinely used his science notebook to take notes and record his ideas while listening to books Mary read aloud to the class during the unit about the environment. He also extended his writing to capture related activities such as when they collected trash from the playground and recycled it. Figure 4.5 displays Cole's notes of main themes, drawing heavily on concepts from the books *The Three Questions* and *Your Environment* to think about what he might recommend for taking care of the environment. Cole and his classmates would later use their notes throughout the unit to begin drafting their class book to share with their kindergarten reading buddies. In this way, the notebook became a tool to help him analyze and synthesize concepts in the unit, and an assessment opportunity for Mary to understand her students' scientific understanding, misconceptions, and ability to record information accurately and systematically.

Using evidence to write informational text

Teachers today consider ways to help their students meet Common Core expectations for using evidence to write informational text, the focus of Common Core Standard 7. This standard requires that students "Participate in shared research and writing projects (e.g., read a number of books on a single topic to produce a report; record science observations)"

Figure 4.4. Robert's Observation Notebook

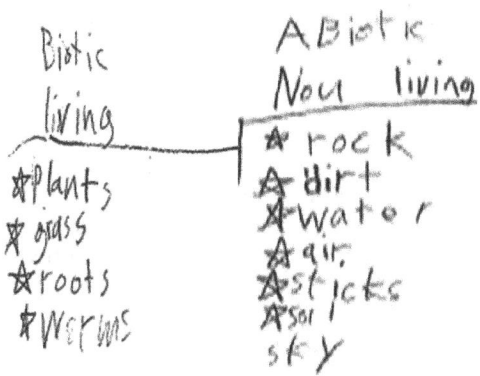

Biotic
living
★plants
★grass
★roots
★worms

ABiotic
Now living
★ rock
★dirt
★water
★air
★sticks
★soil
sky

Figure 4.5. Cole's Science Notebook

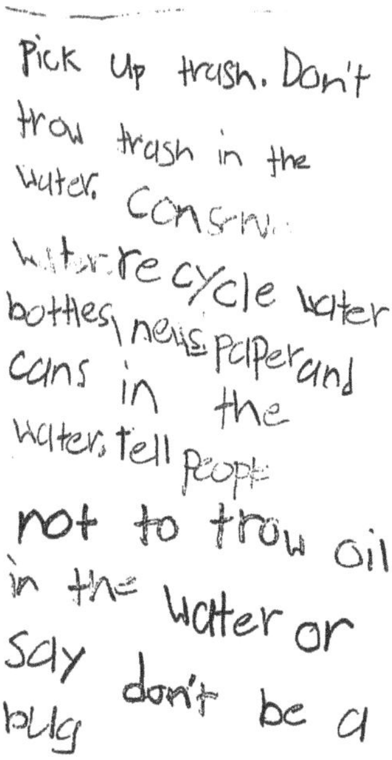

Pick up trash. Don't
trow trash in the
water. Consrv.
watr recycle water
bottles, news paper and
cans in the
water tell people
not to trow oil
in the water or
say don't be a
bug

(CCSS, p. 19). Students learned that to effectively support claims with evidence, they needed to use a broad range of resources to find information about a topic. Mary wanted her students to be well on their way to writing successful informational texts. To help her students write successful informational texts, Mary drew on Marinak and Gambrell's (2009) five teaching elements for nonfiction texts, including author's purpose, major ideas, supporting details, aids (e.g., graphs), and vocabulary.

Using their observational notes during science activities (e.g., Figure 4.4, and their written records of what they learned (e.g., Figure 4.5), Mary's students drew on the evidence they collected to write texts to inform others. As the teacher led small groups in revisiting content from their picture books, observation notebooks, flip charts, and other artifacts from the unit, students learned ways to compile evidence related to their main ideas. For example, Mary met with one small group to review the artifacts and activities about one phase of the unit—becoming aware of and observing our environment. Together, they created a list of topics they had studied. Then, Mary chose one topic and showed the students how to create a graphic organizer of important ideas related to that topic. Next, each student chose one topic from the list they generated, developed his or her own graphic organizer, and used it to write a draft of ideas. Finally, the students collaborated with peers to revise and edit their writing relative to the content they wanted to share and the conventions needed for their audience. Mary used the conversations as a way of assessing students' abilities to engage in substantive writing critiques with peers, as well as their understanding of science concepts.

The classroom writing Mary typically did with her students grew out of their own interests and for audiences of their own choosing. In Mary's unit, students chose their topics (from a list of small-group-generated topics), but the teacher chose the audience. She did so as a way to provide more extensive guidance in introducing new strategies for writing and ensure that students were proficient in writing a variety of texts for many purposes. With kindergartners as the audience, Mary helped her 2nd-grade writers to carefully consider word choices, explain scientific vocabulary, and use text features (e.g., headings, text box), elements (e.g., labels, keys), and format.

To reinforce writing for an external audience, Mary's students read their drafts aloud to each other. Mary guided the listeners to respond first to whether or not the writing made sense. Only then did the students look at the writing together to check for conventions and the effective use of key components of writing. Once the students were confident that their writing made sense and had done their best to address errors in conventions, they met with the teacher to discuss content and final edits. With Mary's approval, they typed their final draft. The completed book served as an authentic assessment of students' understanding of the disciplinary content, as well as their writing abilities. Students had an opportunity to engage in high-level thinking and writing tasks while meeting a real-world demand.

Finally, after printing their text on recycled paper, the students added a picture or other graphics to finalize their contribution to the class book. To help build their fluency with the scientific vocabulary, students practiced reading the class book for several days before reading it to their kindergarten reading buddies.

Examples of Multidisciplinary Writing in 6th Grade

Cassandra integrated writing, in the form of a persuasive letter, into her 6th-grade unit focused on mathematical thinking and problem solving related to budgeting. The letter content drew on what the students learned about budgets, as well as the Internet research they did about school budgets. The authentic audience was a key government or educational official of each student's choice. In creating this unit, Cassandra drew on all five Core Design Principles to set up writing as an integral and critical aspect of learning, one that ultimately included several disciplines such as math, economics, civics, and composition.

Cassandra showed students how often newspaper articles feature budget issues related to a variety of current events (Principle 1). Her instruction about budgets seamlessly dovetailed effective writing strategies and understanding disciplinary concepts. She then helped students develop a point of view on a key issue pertaining to school budgets (Principle 3). She taught them strategies to research sources (including Internet sources) (Principles 2 and 4) and to create convincing arguments in a letter to a government official (Principle 5). Although a focus on budgets might seem a more appropriate concept for older students, keep in mind that even 1st-graders have a lot to say on this issue, extending their concepts of wants versus needs (Gallagher & Hodges, 2010). By 6th grade, the teacher is building on important conceptual conversations from earlier grades.

Learning to be critical consumers of text

Cassandra's goal for the unit was to teach her students how to make decisions about educational budgets and budgeting at the local district and school level. Persuasive letters were the final writing product associated with this overall goal. Students learned how to use a range of resources to write effective persuasive letters. Cassandra had her students write the persuasive letters drawing on processes associated with Common Core Writing Anchor Standard 8: *Gather relevant information from multiple print and digital sources, assess the credibility and accuracy of each source, and integrate the information while avoiding plagiarism.*

In creating the unit, Cassandra helped her students gather information from the Internet, evaluate it for quality/credibility, and then integrate what they learned into their persuasive letters while avoiding plagiarism. She employed the SEARCH strategy as a way of assessing students' ability to judge information. SEARCH is an acronym for a framework that students can apply to informational text (Henry, 2006, p. 618):

1. Set a purpose for searching.
2. Employ effective search strategies.
3. Analyze search engine results.
4. Read critically and synthesize information.
5. Cite your sources.
6. How successful was your search?

To focus students' initial information gathering, Cassandra used this prompt: "Defend or challenge the following statement: 'Media and speakers present factual, unbiased accounts of issues and events.' Be able to explain your answer with examples from your observations and experiences." Cassandra asked her students to share their answers with their table groups. After the students spoke in small groups, the class talked as a whole group and reasoned that bias can exist in a speaker's accounts of events. Roberto gave an example from home. One day he overheard his big brother, Jorge, telling his best friend about an altercation after school, and it sounded like Jorge took quite a beating. When Jorge's mom asked him about his torn shirt that day, however, Jorge said, "It's nothing, Mom. I just got in a scuffle with a friend after school." Roberto said he guessed that Jorge didn't tell their mom the whole story because he didn't want her to go to school and "make a big embarrassing deal about the whole thing."

After discussing Roberto's brother's situation, the group began talking about other examples of biased accounts of stories such as political advertisements on television, and so on. During the discussion, Cassandra continued to ask probing questions, helping the students to see that all human beings have biases. Politicians, news commentators, and the developers of news programs are no different. In fact, others (including politicians, reporters, and news producers) often attempt to persuade audience members to hold particular beliefs about particular subjects and events. Moreover, the language/images that speakers use can impact listeners'/viewers' logic, emotions, and values in order to gain a targeted response.

Cassandra told her students that we live in a world where people are constantly bombarded with information—print, spoken, visual, and auditory, on TV, Internet, radio, social networking sites, Twitter, Facebook, and so forth. Consequently, learning how to evaluate the validity and reliability of the information sources is vital. Cassandra assessed students' ability by having them analyze sources looking for the following information: bias and fairness, context, subtext, and corroboration across sources. Using the set key questions depicted in Figure 4.3 as a guide, Cassandra pulled up the following websites on the whiteboard and entered the search term *education budget cuts*: huffingtonpost.com, drudgereport.com, npr.org, and foxnews.com.

First in small groups, then in the whole group, the class discussed the information provided on each website (e.g., video, photos, blogs, commentary) to determine if the website reported original news or simply posted stories from other websites, and if the site seemed to have a more liberal or conservative viewpoint. Together, Cassandra and her students created a t-chart, which included characteristics of more valid/reliable websites and characteristics of less reliable websites. In the process, Cassandra and her students evaluated each source to determine if it was a primary or secondary source, a key distinction in many disciplines, especially history.

Cassandra also showed students youtube.com and nytimes.com and asked the students to analyze each website using both their list of critical questions (see Figure 4.6) and their criteria t-chart list on quality websites. For each website, the students wondered: *Would you use this website in your research for your letter on budgeting?* The goal was to develop a principled rationale for each answer. Cassandra asked students to continue thinking critically about the information they heard from a variety of media sources and jot down any thoughts or realizations that seemed important.

Writing persuasive letters

Cassandra emphasized writing as a tool used to accomplish civic goals that lead to positive changes in the world. The letters served as authentic assessments of students' ability to research, synthesize information, and write for a specific audience. Maggie Beddow (2012) engaged in a similar project with her bilingual 6th-grade students, where they decided to take

Figure 4.6. Critically Evaluating Online Text

action by writing persuasive letters based on newspaper clippings. Such writing can strongly reinforce the connections between audience and purpose for writing.

Cassandra gave students the option of writing their persuasive letters individually or with a partner. She knew this writing task was particularly complex and challenging and she wanted to give her students the option to collaborate with a peer. She provided support in three ways, including topic selection, audience choice, and scaffolded process writing. First, to help them focus, she encouraged students to prioritize the items about which they felt most strongly and to choose only one or two items to include in their letters. Limiting the number of items helped them to focus their letter and to do careful Internet research to get facts about the implications of budget cuts to the area (e.g., sports, music, art) that mattered to them.

Second, audience matters when writing a persuasive letter. Students considered possible audiences and generated a list that included the state governor, district superintendent, district CFO, school board, and their principal. Students learned about these audiences over the course of the unit since the CFO for the district and the school principal had done guest presentations in their classroom. Each guest speaker mentioned the roles that leaders at various levels play in school and district budgeting decisions. Students had the option of writing to any of the addressees, but they all opted to write to the governor. They articulated their reasons:

- The governor decides how much money to cut from education funds that would go to each school district.
- If the governor cut less money from education for each district, then their superintendent would not need to make the list of cuts he and his group of advisors had proposed.
- The governor's decision regarding overall budget cuts would be finalized in June. If they wrote letters to him immediately as they were engaged in their unit, their voices could be heard at a crucial time.
- The students felt that they could always write to district-level officials later, once final decisions were made about how much money would be budged for their school district.

Thus, although their audience could still change as they wrote their letters, they did have a clear audience in mind. More important, they had a solid sense of why the governor was the best pick for an audience.

Third, similar to Mary's 2nd-graders, the 6th-graders engaged in the process of writing by creating an outline or a concept map based on their research, drafting their letters, revising and editing their letters for content and conventions, and creating final versions of their letters that could be mailed to Governor Sandoval. However, the 6th-graders also spent considerable time independently reading about their topics, drawing on reliable sources from the Internet (e.g., news reports), hearing class speakers (e.g., the school principal and district CFO), and interviewing other educators (e.g., specialist teachers, coaches, classroom teachers). Interviews can be a powerful way for students to connect the past to the present and to understand different perspectives (e.g., Burke, 2011; Jenks, 2010). In gathering information, not only did Cassandra extend students' understanding of primary sources (e.g., interview experts, websites), but she taught them how to recognize perspectives from a range of sources and give credit to sources, including direct quotes.

Examples of persuasive letters

The 6th-graders' letters generally focused on three topics: (1) budget impacts on reduction of teachers; (2) budget impact on sports, music, or art programs; and (3) potential closing of schools. In Figure 4.7, Shakia's letter draws on various facts and information about the benefits of sports and the potential impact of program cuts on her own athletic and physical development. Though she gives clear references to the people she interviewed, she still needs to learn how to cite sources to support the factual information she gathered. In Figure 4.8, Bonita also draws on information she gathered on the impact of teacher layoffs and class sizes, giving information from related projects and programs. In both letters, the students showed their developing knowledge of how to write a letter intended to persuade another person, including sharing their own point of view on the issues.

EXAMINING CLASSROOM WRITING ACROSS DISCIPLINES

In the examples from Mary's and Cassandra's rooms, writing is an integral component of helping the students think about what they are learning and how to share that information with various audiences. As you pull together the instructional frameworks and examples provided, consider three key ideas about writing that can support your disciplinary literacy instruction.

1. Writing can serve as a tool to understand disciplinary concepts, including how disciplinary experts use writing in particular ways. In these examples, students had a clear sense of an audience beyond their classroom, one that likely increased their engagement with writing and their efforts to clearly convey their new conceptual knowledge. It is still critically important for students to write fiction as well, though extending to nonfiction, primary sources, and digital media helps them to further learn the content of each discipline.

2. Students need to learn to use a range of resources to compose arguments, support claims, and meet other goals of writing texts. Using mentor picture books, Internet sources, interviews with experts, and observation notes, students wrote informational texts and persuasive letters relevant to concepts associated with science and math. Just as students need to read different types of texts pertinent to the disciplines, they need to write these texts as well.

3. Assessments have to reflect the different types of composing process-es students will use in real-world settings. Assessment should include eval-uation of students' finished texts, as well as the writing process. Multigenre writing (Romano, 2000) is an effective assessment of student learning in the disciplines, as it encompasses research, content, and various types of texts that reflect authentic tasks outside of school.

Figure 4.7. Shakia's Persuasive Letter

June 2, 2011

Dear Governor Sandoval,

I am a 6th grader from Rockland Elementary School in the Nevada County School District. I have seven brothers and one sister. I grew up with boys, and I have spent time playing activities like playing soccer, basketball, and also not cleaning my room! I'm 12 years old, and I teach my brothers what I have learned from school.

In school, I have learned about budget cuts. Our principal told us how she creates her budget for everything that our school needs. I've heard that you are going to cut off the budget so much it could cut off school sports. I'm writing this letter to persuade you not to cut school sports.

The physical benefits of sports are that it helps children reduce weight; lower weight can help children not get the 2 types of diabetes. Type 2 diabetes is currently a serious health issue to America's obese children. Sports can help improve the 5 components of fitness namely: strength speed, skill, stamina, and suppleness. Sports can burn calories and affect your appetite. Sports keep you active everyday and keep you out of trouble.

The social benefits of sports are that 50% of non-sport participants drop out of school by the time they reach early adolescence. Female high school athletes are 92% less likely to get involved with drugs. High school athletes in North Carolina make higher grades, get into less trouble, graduate at a higher rate, drop out less often, and have higher GPAs than non-athletes. Also, sports keep teens from using drugs. Girls who play different kinds of sports are less likely to have a baby.

When asked if they felt sports should be cut, Mrs. Cagney said, "No, sports are a very important part of a child's education. There are both physical and social benefits to playing sports." Dr. Brock said, "No, because it is important to keep sports in schools. Athletics benefit children physically and socially." Mrs. Wolter said that "cutting all sports would get parents' attention and probably encourage them to support new taxes, so even though I believe in sports in education in general—it is the first thing I would cut to make a point. It is a school district, not a play district."

In my opinion, I think it should not be cut because sports are really important to kids. I believe that if sports were cut from my education, I would be missing out on the physical and social benefits of sports. I hope my opinion will change your opinion.

Sincerely, Shakia

Figure 4.8. Bonita's Persuasive Letter
_____

June 2, 2011

Dear Governor Sandoval,

   I am a 6th grade student from Rockland Elementary in the Nevada County School District [pseudonym] in Reno, NV. I've been learning about budget cuts and how they affect people. Our principal, Mrs. Smith [pseudonym], came to our classroom and talked about school budget cuts. Mrs. Smith said that in the last two years she let two teachers go. But this year she has to let go two more teachers and a helper.

   Increasing class sizes could cause students to fall behind, and students are dropping out because teachers don't talk to them individually, and the students get lost because they don't understand. Smaller class sizes cause students' grades to go up, which is what we want to happen. In Indiana, many first graders showed growth instead of a flat line after students were put in smaller classes (Indiana's Time Prime Project). Achievement Programs found that students in smaller classes improved their grades.

   Getting prepared to lay off teachers is one of the terrible things the budget cuts could do. If the school district doesn't get the money it has requested, teachers will probably get laid off. Charlotte Mecklenburg School District in North Carolina wants 50 million extra dollars to help TA'S and other programs and classrooms, like getting the supplies that programs need. This is not what Nevada is asking. Our school district isn't asking for extra money; it's just asking to not be cut so that education is negatively impacted.

   Trying to convince the school district to not lay off teachers requires that you provide enough money through the budget to fund teachers. Thank you for considering my request.

Sincerely, Bonita
_____

CHAPTER 5

Disciplinary Literacy and Classroom Talk

Cynthia Brock, Kathryn Obenchain, Taffy Raphael,
Catherine Weber, Elisabeth Trost-Shahata, and Virginia Goatley

Talk is at the heart of classroom teaching and learning (Boyd & Galda, 2011; Gee, 2012). When teachers engage students in meaningful conversations and encourage students to talk with each other, they set a context for deep conceptual learning (Wells, 2009). In this chapter, we explore the pivotal role talk plays in disciplinary learning. Within the disciplines, a focus on classroom talk is particularly important for understanding difficult vocabulary, developing conceptual knowledge, and learning to read and write in discipline-specific ways. Using talk in meaningful ways in the disciplines aligns with Common Core standards that emphasize the importance of disciplinary learning. To help you create effective instruction using talk in your classroom, we provide examples of how students use talk in classrooms as Elisabeth and Mary teach their students social studies and scientific concepts. Figure 5.1 describes talk in terms of the Core Design Principles described in Chapter 1.

WHAT MATTERS ABOUT CLASSROOM TALK

Classroom talk is a critical component of disciplinary learning because much of what we learn, we learn through speaking and listening. In this chapter, we present four components of a coherent instructional framework for using talk in the classroom: (1) Talk plays a central role in learning, (2) classrooms have meaningful and engaging talk, (3) norms for talk vary by culture and discipline, and (4) assessment should be focused on meaningful talk.

Figure 5.1. Core Design Principles for Talk

Design Principle	Example
1. Authentic Social and Cultural Practices	Use talk as a tool to engage in discipline-specific discourse practices (e.g., engaging in deliberation, seminar, and conversation so as to foster effective ways of *knowing* and *being* together).
2. Optimal Learning Model	Use talk as a tool to engage in scaffolding disciplinary understandings (e.g., to help children learn to build theories and then evaluate those theories based on evidence, and/or help children develop new conceptual understandings—such as developing historical empathy).
3. Key Inquiry Questions	Use inquiry to drive questioning and research to learn new concepts (e.g., to develop understandings of historical events, scientific processes, and so on).
4. Composing Requires a Range of Resources	Teach children to draw on resources such as read-alouds, artifacts, Internet research, and interviews with experts.
5. Authentic Assessments Reflect Meaning-Making Process	Use performance assessments to monitor the nature of children's talk as they engage in discipline-specific activities.

Component One: Talk Plays a Central Role in Learning

Talk is a central tool for learning. We develop content knowledge through social interaction and suitable scaffolding, typically involving talking, listening, and doing. We learn to read, write, talk, and listen in particular ways within each discipline (Vygotsky, 1978; Wells, 2009). For example, if you have ever read (or written) a legal document, you know such documents are written in unique ways and serve unique purposes (e.g., wills, real estate transactions, and so forth). Even if one is highly educated in a nonlegal profession, it can be difficult to understand legal documents without a lawyer to translate and explain what they mean. The same is true for disciplinary teaching and learning. Scientists, mathematicians, and historians use talk in unique ways to develop content knowledge. Our task as teachers is twofold, to help our students (1) learn to use talk in discipline-specific ways and (2) learn disciplinary content through talk (Moje, 2010; Shanahan & Shanahan, 2012).

Component Two: Meaningful Talk in a Variety of Settings

Classrooms should be engaging places where meaningful, educative talk is prevalent within and across disciplines—among teachers and children and within various arrangements of children (whole-group talk, paired talk, small-group talk, and so on). Engaging in disciplinary talk is critical for college and career readiness, as illustrated by Britton's celebrated statement "our lives are afloat on a sea of talk" (quoted in Judy, 1974, p. 187). Matz Rosen (1992) argues that our classrooms should be afloat on a sea of talk where teachers and students use language to "to share ideas, to discover ideas, to chat and to record, to solve problems and to respond to issues, to gather new information and to share what has already been learned" (p. 10). Classrooms "afloat on a sea of talk" are consistent with the Common Core speaking and listening standards, where productive talk prepares students to participate effectively in "a range of conversations and collaborations with diverse partners, building on others' ideas and expressing their own clearly and persuasively" (CCSS, 2010, p. 22). Further, teachers make numerous important decisions about language choices, instructional words, and supportive talk to facilitate student learning (Johnston, 2004; Lindfors, 2008; Wells, 2009), within and across disciplines.

Component Three: Norms for Talk Vary by Culture and Discipline

The norms for how people engage in talk vary from group to group. Teachers can provide effective disciplinary literacy instruction if they (1) recognize that conversational norms vary and (2) vary classroom activities and participation structures so students can learn about disciplinary content and processes.

Conversational norms vary among different groups

Have you ever been in a conversation with a student or a parent where you found it difficult to express your ideas or understand the other person's ideas? There are many different norms for talk within various groups (e.g., ethnic background) and disciplines (e.g., how scientists and historians talk with one another). For example, extensive scholarship has shown how talk between teachers and children from different ethnic groups can vary in ways that impact children's learning. Au (1980) found that when teachers of Native Hawaiian children used a "talk story" (an approach to talk that is familiar to Native Hawaiian children), the children were more successful literacy learners. Similarly, Philips (1983) studied the nature of communication among Indians in the Warm Springs Tribe in Central Oregon, while also studying the transition of children from Warm Springs to Anglo schools. Philips found that the purposes, cultural norms, and communication styles between the Warm Springs Indians and the Anglo teachers in local schools were vastly different. When Anglo teachers recognized these differences and sought to build a bridge between communication norms, Warm Springs children were more successful in school.

Just as norms for talk can vary between ethnic groups, norms for talk also vary within different disciplines (Shanahan & Shanahan, 2008). For example, when studying a historical event, historians must draw on a range of artifacts to craft well-reasoned arguments for their interpretation of the event. They must provide evidence, in forms that are acceptable to other historians, to support the assertions and interpretations of the historical event. Scientists use talk to pose questions, construct plausible explanations to answer their questions, test their explanations using approaches that are acceptable to other scientists, and then communicate their findings in their scientific communities.

Varying classroom participation structures

There are many ways to organize classroom interactions, including whole groups, small groups, and dyads to foster disciplinary literacy learning. Whole-group instruction has been a long-standing way to organize classroom interactions, with the Initiate-Respond-Evaluate (IRE) being a traditional communication pattern during whole-group instruction (Cazden, 2001). During instruction, the teacher *initiates* conversation with a question; students raise their hands, vying for the conversational floor, and the teacher chooses a child to *respond*; then, the teacher *evaluates* the child's response. The teacher does most of the talking within the IRE pattern of communication.

There are many times when it is important for teachers to use whole-group approaches during instruction (Wells, 2009). A teacher can use whole-group time to build shared understandings of disciplinary concepts and ideas. Additionally, teachers can model important speaking and listening skills emphasized in the CCSS. For example, when drawing on multiple sources to craft an argument about a historical event, a teacher can model how to express ideas clearly and persuasively.

However, students also need opportunities to engage in meaningful and educative talk with peers in small groups and dyads. This gives students opportunities to sort through and explore conceptual ideas. For example, Ilene Berson's (2009) 6- and 7-year-old children worked in small groups to create podcasts to present their learning of social studies concepts. While developing the podcasts, Ilene's children deepened their understanding of social studies content and processes. This type of small-group instruction gives teachers the chance to enact CCSS speaking and listening standards, including "presenting information, findings, and supporting evidence such that listeners can follow the line of reasoning" (CCSS, p. 22) as well as "using digital media to express information and enhance understanding" (p. 22).

Component Four: Assessment Focused on Meaningful Talk

Assessment should reflect how children use talk to construct meaning about the disciplines. In your classroom, do you assess how students speak and listen? In many classrooms, assessing how students speak and listen is rarely a priority for assessment or something that is represented on report cards. However, it is a critical pathway into how students think and express their ideas. Classroom talk provides teachers with information about students' abilities to talk within a community of learners and make meaning across the curriculum (e.g., social studies, science, literature). Like other areas of literacy (e.g., reading, writing), classroom talk should be assessed strategically and systematically. Assessments will reflect the different ways children use talk to learn if teachers do the following: (1) Use assessments to understand how students interact with one another, (2) audio- and/or videotape conversations to analyze later, and (3) encourage students to keep a notebook of their developing ideas over time and use the notations as a basis for discussion with their peers.

Assess how students interact with one another

In social studies classrooms, assessment should focus on students' abilities to interact with one another in a community of learners and demonstrate what they know about the content (Parker & Hess, 2001). To assess students' abilities to interact well with others, you can create a checklist for purposeful observation that includes items such as *stays on topic, asks relevant questions, respects others, collaborates, synthesizes information from multiple sources,* and *uses academic vocabulary.* Because it is difficult to observe all students at once, plan to focus on a few students each day and systematically record information about their classroom talk. Then, you will be in a better position to draw on what they know to inform instruction for the next day. Over time, you will have detailed records for each of the students over several days of their participation and will be able to track their individual development.

Analyze audio/videotape talk

Assessing classroom talk can be challenging, particularly when the teacher is part of the conversation with the students. For example, you will read about Elisabeth's use of a three-pronged approach to classroom discussion (i.e., develop conceptual understandings, deliberate and construct arguments, and reach consensus) with her 4th-graders. One of the most effective ways to assess classroom talk is to audio- or videotape discussions to analyze later. This allows you to assess students, as well as become more aware of how you respond to individuals. Ideas to consider when analyzing the video include, but are not limited to: the purpose of the conversation, ratio of talk (student-student and student-teacher), elaboration of ideas, negotiations and/or debates, and feedback (about content or group interactions).

   Analysis of teacher talk should focus on the opportunities provided for students to engage in deliberation (deciding on the means to achieve a goal), seminar (using talk to facilitate understanding), and conversation (talk to reach consensus). Analysis of student talk should focus on ways in which the students engage with others when given the opportunity. You can use this information about classroom talk to strategically plan instruction that addresses content and citizenship in the social studies classroom.

Analyze student progress portfolio

Assessment in the science classroom should include information gathering about students' abilities to engage in the social process of science (Lemke, 2000), as well as the content (e.g., reasoning, observing, analyzing). Emphasis should be placed on students' developing scientific thinking, not simply getting the "right" answer. An effective way to measure students' abilities in this area is through a growth and learning progress portfolio (see Nitko, 1996). In their portfolio, students maintain documents that represent their learning.

   One part of the portfolio is a notebook that students keep to trace their developing ideas across time. They use notations in their notebooks as a basis for discussion with their teacher and peers. Teachers' analyses of the growth and learning progress portfolio should focus on students' understandings, strategies for solving problems, and patterns of thinking.

For example, you will read about how Mary's students used inquiry to conduct investigations and experiments. During such inquiry, students use their notebooks to record thoughts or questions about text they read, hypotheses, trial and error, metacognitive processes, and so forth. Additionally, teachers should have students use their notebooks to record changes in thinking as a result of engaging in discussion with other scientists in the classroom. The growth and learning progress portfolio provides a window into what students are thinking, how thinking changes over time, and how classroom talk influences their abilities to engage in scientific inquiry.

DISCIPLINARY LITERACY AND CLASSROOM TALK

To help you get started on transforming your classroom to include talk as a tool for disciplinary learning, we share examples of classroom talk from Elisabeth's 4th- and Mary's 2nd-grade classrooms, embedded within their themes on *why we remember Sacagawea* and *caring for the environment*, respectively. One of their goals is that students learn about the purposes and functions that talk serves in different disciplines. In Elisabeth's 4th-grade classroom, students use talk to (1) develop understandings of social studies (e.g., history, citizenship education, economics, geography) concepts such as cultural universals, historical empathy, and habits of mind required to be informed members of a democracy; (2) deliberate and construct arguments; and (3) reach consensus.

Mary uses talk as a tool with her 2nd-graders to (1) develop understandings of scientific concepts and processes (e.g., scientific inquiry), and (2) engage in scientific argumentation. Each of the examples that follow illustrates three key ideas about disciplinary literacy instruction: (1) that talk is a tool for understanding disciplinary concepts, (2) that students need to learn to use talk in different ways for different disciplinary purposes, and (3) that assessments must reflect different uses of talk for real-world settings and purposes.

Examples of Classroom Talk During 4th-Grade Social Studies

Elisabeth drew on the five design principles introduced in Chapter 1 for her unit. Elisabeth's unit question "Why should we remember Sacagawea?" provided a way for thinking about all aspects of the unit instruction (Guiding Principle 3). Throughout the unit, Elisabeth supported her students' use of talk (Principle 2) in meaningful ways (Principle 1) using a range of resources

(Principle 4) in the form of different books and activities to help her students explore Sacagawea's life and experiences. Additionally, Elisabeth used authentic assessments (Principle 5) to document her students' learning across time as the unit unfolded.

Elisabeth is aware that classroom talk serves unique purposes and functions in social studies. For example, effective classroom talk in social studies can apprentice students into "ways of *knowing* and ways of *being* together" (Parker & Hess, 2001, p. 273, emphasis added). As students develop both the knowledge and habits of mind required to be active and informed members of a democracy, they are apprenticed into *ways of knowing. Ways of being together* refers to "the pedagogical aim of creating vigorous communities of inquiry" (p. 273). To be productive members of a democracy, citizens need to acquire knowledge about citizenship as well as learn how citizens act and interact together in effective ways. The three examples that follow illustrate how Elisabeth used talk with her students to help them develop understandings of historical concepts, to deliberate and develop arguments, and to reach consensus.

Using talk to develop understandings of social studies concepts

Elisabeth varied the forms of talk that she used throughout the unit. As she introduced social studies concepts at the beginning of the unit, talk occurred in a whole-group setting while students sat in a large circle with copies of the anchor text *Who Was Sacagawea?* (Fradin & Fradin, 2002). Elisabeth used an IRE (Initiate-Respond-Evaluate) pattern of talk to overview text features in the first chapter and model ways to interpret them in light of important historical concepts such as cultural universals. Cultural universals—which include the need for food, clothing, and shelter—are "domains of human experience that have existed for all cultures, past and present" (Brophy & Alleman, 2006, p. 5). Elisabeth knows that text features such as text boxes in informational texts often highlight important disciplinary content (Derewianka & Jones, 2012). Pointing to a text box that provides the reader with background information about buffalo hunting, Elisabeth read, "Before Europeans first started settling in America, there were over 50,000,000 buffalo and the Native Americans relied heavily on the buffalo for food, shelter, and clothing" (Fradin & Fradin, 2002, p. 8). Elisabeth highlighted the importance of information that is conveyed through text features beyond connected prose (e.g., text boxes). Then she posed questions about the feature she had just shared (*initiate*). The questions focused students' attention on two aspects. One set of questions she asked focused their attention on the feature (e.g., "What do you notice about how the text box is organized? How does that help you know what information is important? Why do you think the author chose to share the information in this way?"). The other set of questions focused students' attention on the content (e.g., "What does this text box tell us about why buffalo were so important to Native Americans?").

Following each question, Elisabeth asked her students to take turns *responding*. Sometimes she commented on their responses, while at other times, she invited multiple responses before moving on to the final phase of the IRE. In her *evaluation*, Elisabeth analyzed students' responses to determine their understanding of the information she had just shared with them—both the feature and its form and function and the content conveyed through the feature. Using talk in this manner, Elisabeth made visible to her students the three cultural universals (e.g., the notion that all humans need food, shelter, and clothing) central to understanding the circumstances of Sacagawea's time and place in history.

The talk in which Elisabeth and her students engaged about cultural universals provided the foundation for guiding students' learning about historical empathy (Seixas, 1993). Historical empathy is the ability to empathize with a person or group from history and their experiences, *while understanding the historical, political, sociocultural, and economic context in which they lived*. Thus, after discussing the text box about buffalo hunting, Elisabeth asked her students to talk with a partner to "think about *how Sacagawea might have felt* to see the destruction of the buffalo." Notice that Elisabeth asked her students how *Sacagawea* might have felt rather than how *they* might have felt. This is an important distinction for developing historical empathy.

Elisabeth understands that historical empathy is not about asking students to "think how you would feel if this happened to you." Historians recognize that historical contexts are often too different from modern-day contexts. The majority of us are unlikely to be able to imagine the different kinds of experiences that some groups of people have encountered. As one extreme example, most of us would have no way of being able to understand what it would be like to be a victim of genocide. Rather, Elisabeth's approach encouraged the students to consider the context in which Sacagawea lived. By examining how humans address common experiences (e.g., the need for food, shelter, and clothing) in another time and/or place, the students made connections to current-day needs for food, shelter, and clothing.

From their discussion in the whole group (primarily using an IRE pattern of talk) as well as through Elisabeth's asking the students to engage in dyad discussions, the students learned that by the late 1800s the buffalo was an endangered species. White buffalo hunters had slaughtered most of the buffalo living in the Great Plains. Only 550 buffalo remained, and the Native Americans depended upon them for their survival. This buffalo slaughtering had a devastating effect on Native Americans who relied on the animal for food, clothing, and shelter. During this discussion, Elisabeth asked: "How do you think that the Native Americans felt when their sources of food, clothing, and shelter were taken away?" Layla responded, "I think that they were sad and angry. . . . (T)hey were worried about how they would live."

Providing scaffolding for constructing a viable argument (CCSS Speaking & Listening Standard 4), Elisabeth showed Layla and her classmates what evidence from the text she could draw on to support her interpretation. Elisabeth explained that according to their text, buffalo were the Native Americans' main source of food, clothing, and shelter. Elisabeth then pointed to several specific examples from the text illustrating how the Native Americans used buffalo for food, clothing, and shelter. Thus, through her varied use of talk during instruction, Elisabeth modeled how to take into account social studies concepts (cultural universals and historical empathy) and use them to engage in the language of historians (constructing disciplinary arguments).

For more information about how you can engage students through the meaningful use of talk to teach important social studies concepts in your own classroom, go to the following link at the website for the National Council for Social Studies (NCSS): http://www.socialstudies.org/standards/strands. This link takes you directly to the "Ten Themes of Social Studies" on the NCSS website. Also at the main link for the NCSS website (http://www.socialstudies.org/), you will find countless resources for using talk in meaningful ways to teach social studies in your own classroom.

Using talk to reach consensus

As Elisabeth continued to teach social studies concepts, vocabulary, and historical content and processes during the unit, she created opportunities to teach basic strategies that are useful to learning in social studies. For example, it is critical to understand conceptually what a main idea is, and how details support a main idea. Such understandings are central to creating an effective argument. Thus, Elisabeth explained and modeled talk about main ideas and details as students read Sacagawea's biography and created timelines of her life.

Elisabeth paid particular attention to her English learners because she has found that distinguishing between main ideas and supporting details can be difficult for English learners who may still be focusing their attention at the word level. Using a section of the book to illustrate how to determine the difference between main ideas and details, Elisabeth's talk took the form of a think-aloud, making visible specific characteristics of main ideas (e.g., in biographies main ideas are often tied to events, and events in the text may differ in their impact on Sacagawea's life) and details (information that helps readers understand an event, such as when it took place, how old Sacagawea was, the kinds of changes the event led to in her life). This explicit modeling provided Elisabeth's students with examples of the kinds of talk she wanted her students to appropriate in their own small-group discussions (Guiding Principle 2: Scaffolding).

After using talk to model for her students the distinction between main ideas and details in Sacagawea's life, Elisabeth asked them to talk in their small, peer-led discussion groups to reach consensus about the main event(s) in one of the book chapters and the supporting details that provided useful information about that event. For example, in the excerpt below, the students discussed what they considered to be the main events in Chapter 3, in which the biography described Sacagawea's role in the ongoing journey west. Using markers and a half-sheet of chart paper, they discussed in small groups to reach consensus, first about what the main event was, and then about the important details that helped them understand the event and its importance. In Vanessa's group, the following conversation ensued:

Vanessa: Okay, we have to find the main events.
José: The winter of 1804 was very cold.
Syed: That's not a main event.

[Commentary: Vanessa is using language that Elisabeth modeled in the whole group, specifically adopting the word main to describe events. Syed repeats the word main, emphasizing the word event in his somewhat abrupt criticism of José. Then, Layla builds on this concept by providing an example of an event that was central to the chapter.]

Layla: What about when Sacagawea saved the supplies when the boat turned over?
Vanessa: Yeah, that's definitely a main event because it's really important.

[Commentary: Vanessa's initial definition of the main event in accepting Layla's suggestion is essentially circular reasoning—it's

*"main" because it's "important"—and is challenged by José. She
then tries to expand by contrasting an event with a fact or detail (i.e.,
weather). In her response, she appropriates Elisabeth's language that
an event is "something that happens."]*

José: Why can't we use my example?

Layla: . . . because an event is something that happened. That isn't an
  event. It is telling us about the weather.

José: Ohhh . . . okay. So when the boat turned over, Sacagawea saved
  the supplies. That is something that happened.

Layla: Yeah, and the reason it's a main event is because they couldn't
  have continued on the trip without supplies.

The excerpt above illustrates how the students use talk to build consensus,
using their understanding of main ideas and details to identify (1) events and
(2) their importance. It also illustrates how students can use talk to provide
concrete examples to support their positions (such as Layla and José's example of discussing the difference between an event and a detail and why an
event is a main event).

Elisabeth noted that the exchange above illustrated how, through evidence-based respectful speaking and listening (Parker & Hess, 2001), the
students in José's group came to consensus on what counted as an event,
leading them eventually to construct an argument about which event in
this chapter was most important to Sacagawea during this time period.
Discussions such as this excerpt continued until the students in each group
completed, on large chart paper, their lists about the main events in the
chapter and their importance to Sacagawea's life.

Using talk to deliberate, construct arguments, and reach consensus

In addition to using talk to teach her students to reach consensus, Elisabeth
emphasized the importance of using talk *to deliberate during discussions.*
Building on the activity described in the section above, Elisabeth collected
each group's chart paper. She then had students "number off" in a jigsaw
style, forming new groups with no more than two of the same people from
any original group. She distributed a list to each new group with colored
markers. She directed the new groups to deliberate about the events listed
on the chart paper they were given (Were the events "main" ones? Were
these main events equally important to Sacagawea's life?). Students engaged
in considerable negotiation as they referred to the chart paper lists and
weighed the ideas listed.

For example, Omar's group engaged in debate, negotiating the difference between simply correctly being listed as an event and being a *main* event in Sacagawea's life. This process provided an authentic opportunity for the students to state claims and provide evidence to support their claims, an ability stressed in the Common Core. Omar read the following sentence aloud: "The expedition continued on April 7." Then, the following exchange occurred:

> *Omar:* One of our main events is that the expedition continued on April 7.
>
> *Jacqueline:* You're right, that's an event, but in my group we said that was not a main event.
>
> *Emmanuel:* Is it more important to know that the expedition continued, or is it more important to know that Sacagawea saved the supplies when the boat turned over?

> *[Commentary: Emmanuel poses a reasonable question designed to tease out the difference between an event and a main event. His talk focuses his peers' attention on weighing what is more important. His use of a question is a feature of deliberation that Elisabeth had modeled during whole-group instruction within the IRE pattern of talk.]*

> *Jacqueline:* Our group thought it was more important that she saved the supplies because everyone knows the expedition continued. If she didn't save the supplies, the expedition would have ended.

> *[Commentary: Jacqueline emphasizes that one event (saving the supplies) is subordinate to why saving them was important—the expedition needed supplies to continue.]*

Elisabeth's analysis of such talk allowed her to determine the amount of uptake from her modeling. She noted, for example, that Emmanuel's question to conceptually push his classmates' thinking provided evidence that he had begun to internalize the construct of deliberation, which is central to being a productive member of a democracy (Parker & Hess, 2001).

Conversations such as these illustrate how students at different levels in Elisabeth's classroom were able to participate productively. For example, in José's group, part of the conversation focused on what constituted an event. The more sophisticated conversation in Emmanuel's group reflected students distinguishing between chapter events and main events in the life of the subject of the biography. An important feature of these small-group conversations was that the students talked through social studies concepts and processes based on their current levels of conceptual understandings and needs.

Following their deliberations, the various groups presented their revised charts in a whole-class setting. Elisabeth and her students reached consensus about the most significant events. As the class engaged in this process, Elisabeth was careful to point out the connection between the process they had engaged in and the work of historians. She reminded them that historians, authors, thinkers, and writers must decide what they consider most significant and then present evidence to support their assertions. Through their discussion, they experienced how historians may select different events as significant, depending on their individual perspectives.

The students engaged in deliberation as they debated in their small groups to reach consensus about what constitutes a main idea and what constitutes a supporting detail in their reading and how that informs their thinking about the subject of the biography. Students engaged in deliberation once they were regrouped, this time responding to their peers' analyses. When each group presented its revised determination for its last negotiation, the class had another opportunity to engage in deliberation. In each of these cases, the students used talk to deliberate, construct reasoned arguments, and achieve their goal of reaching consensus.

Even very young children can learn to use talk to problem-solve, explain and justify their positions, and reach consensus. For example, Barnes, Johnson, and Neff (2010) shared how a group of 1st-graders used "process drama" to explore "economic wants, resources, scarcity, allocate resources . . ." and so forth in their study of government (p. 19). Studying student dialogue in the unit, the authors found that the students learned effective problem-solving skills and were able to explain and justify their reasoning for decisions they made as they enacted scenarios during the drama component of the unit.

Examples of Classroom Talk During 2nd-Grade Science

Talk serves unique functions and purposes during social studies lessons, as well as during science lessons (Gallas, 1995). Scientists highlight two important points about talk in science. First, science involves a set of social practices unique to scientific communities (Design Principle 1: Authentic Social & Cultural Practices). As such, according to Lemke (2000, emphasis added):

> Whenever we do science, we take ways of talking, reasoning, observing, analyzing, and writing that we have learned from our community and use them to

construct findings and arguments that become part of science only when they become shared in that community. *Teaching science is teaching students how to do science.* Teaching, learning, and doing science are all social processes: taught, learned, and done as members of social communities, small (like classrooms) and large. (p. xi)

Second, since science is a shared set of social practices among scientists, students benefit when their teachers model and help students understand norms (i.e., ways of talking, reasoning, observing, analyzing, reading, and writing) of the scientific community (Design Principle 2: Scaffolding). Lemke (2000) argues that science teachers already speak and understand the language of science. Teachers draw on this knowledge to scaffold children's learning to talk, read, and write like scientists.

What are important norms of science talk and what do these norms look like in practice? Mary's science unit in her 2nd-grade classroom focused on caring for soil, land, and water. Examples from Mary's unit illustrate how she used talk herself and created opportunities for her students to use talk to (1) develop understandings of scientific concepts and inquiry processes and (2) engage in scientific argumentation.

Exploring scientific concepts and processes

Mary knows that inquiry serves as an important foundation in teaching science. According to the Next Generation Science Standards (2011):

The learning experiences provided for students should engage them with fundamental questions about the world and with how scientists have investigated and found answers to those questions. Throughout the K–12 grades, students should have the opportunity to carry out scientific investigations and engineer design projects related to the disciplinary core ideas. (p. 1.2)

Mary knows that scientists conduct investigations and experiments using an inquiry approach. Thus, unlike direct instruction, in which the teacher delivers content through lecture, demonstrations, and directed learning (and children passively follow directions), inquiry teaching requires students to discover phenomena through experiences that require critical thinking and problem solving.

During inquiry instruction, "students describe objects and events, ask questions, construct explanations, test those explanations against current scientific knowledge, and communicate their ideas to others. They identify their assumptions, use critical and logical thinking, and consider alternative explanations" (National Research Council [NRC], 2012, p. 2). Teachers who assume an inquiry stance take a facilitator role as they use talk to guide students to explore the phenomena under investigation.

At the end of the first part of her unit, Mary enacted a series of activities that comprised five phases of scientific inquiry. Mary's overall goal was to use the inquiry process to help children explore the impact of pollution on our environment. This series of inquiry lessons involved guiding the children to discover components of the environment and the differences between a "clean" and "polluted" environment. We present the series of phases to illustrate the considerable time Mary spent using meaningful talk to socialize her students into the scientific inquiry process.

Scientific inquiry: Getting children engaged

Mary used talk with her students to engage in scientific inquiry and meaningfully explore science concepts (NRC, 2012). Mary knows that read-alouds are a great way to use the language of science to get children interested in science concepts, so she gathered her class in a small circle on the floor and read aloud the book *I Took a Walk* (Cole, 1998). The focus of her talk during the read-aloud was guiding the children to notice differences between living (biotic) and nonliving (abiotic) things. Mary used the whole-group IRE (Initiate-Respond-Evaluate) pattern of talk paired with dyad talk during the read-aloud. For example, after reading a few pages about what the bears encountered on their walk, Mary asked children to talk with a partner about the different living and nonliving things that the bears in the text encountered during their walk. Then, after the children talked briefly with their partners, Mary asked selected dyads to respond aloud in the whole group. Mary evaluated their talk to make sure they understood the difference between living and nonliving things. Mary engaged her students with scientific content and the science-related processes of posing questions and constructing explanations through her use of whole-group and paired talk during the read-aloud.

Scientific inquiry: Exploration

Using talk in small groups and the whole group, Mary taught her children to explore and classify, both of which are important components of the scientific inquiry process (NRC, 2012). After discussing *I Took a Walk* (Cole,

1998) with the children, Mary asked them to share in groups of four to explore and classify the differences between living and nonliving things. Because Mary had modeled how to use talk to pose questions and provide evidence while crafting scientific explanations during the read-aloud, her use of talk served as a scaffold for ways the children could use talk in their small groups as they engaged in scientific exploration.

Mary distributed a mini-environment tub containing soil, earthworms, plants, rocks, flowers, and so on to each group with directions to explore the tubs together. As the children created t-charts in their individual science logs to record the (living) biotic and (nonliving) abiotic items from their mini-environment tubs, Mary reminded them that they would be sharing their findings with their peers; consequently, they needed to be prepared to use talk to justify the writing in their t-charts.

When the children shared their lists on their t-charts with peers in their respective groups, Juan noticed that Chris, one of his tablemates, had listed plants under the abiotic category. Juan asked Chris why he listed plants as abiotic. Chris explained, "Because plants can't move." Juan, Chris, and the other children discussed the fact that not all living things move. Thus, the other children in his group used talk in a meaningful way to (1) explore and classify living and nonliving things, and (2) help Chris better understand what is biotic and abiotic, and the kinds of items that should be classified as either living or nonliving. Mary was happy as she overheard the children in this group talking. She realized that they were appropriating the science language and concepts she had modeled in the whole group as they talked with their peers.

Scientific inquiry: Explanation

Scientists explain phenomena (NRC, 2012), and Mary used talk to teach her children to do this, too. In the first two activities, Mary introduced her children to the components of an ecosystem. Then, she "built out" conceptually to help her children explore how the different pieces come together to make up an ecosystem. After convening her children on the rug in a whole group, Mary reproduced a blank t-chart with only the headers *biotic* and *abiotic*. She used a combination of a whole-group IRE pattern of talk, with dyad conversations embedded, so that she could model the use of scientific concepts and processes. She asked the children to share their observations and notes from their science logs as she recorded them on the group's t-chart. Mary also added the words *biotic* and *abiotic* to the class word wall.

Armed with important knowledge of scientific concepts that are a part of an ecosystem, Mary read aloud from the nonfiction text *Your Environment* (Williams, 1998) to introduce two concepts: *environment* and *ecosystem*. As Mary read the story aloud, she posed questions and led a discussion using key questions to guide the children's attention to key environmental contexts: What makes up the land? Where do you find water? Where is the air? How do you know? As she finished reading the book, she asked children if and how people might harm their environment. Then, she gave them a few moments to talk with a partner to share their thoughts and hunches with one another. Asking several dyads of children to share their thoughts and hunches aloud with the whole group (*initiate*), the children *responded*. Mary then *evaluated* their contributions, shaping them to describe scientific concepts and processes using scientific discourse. Here, Mary is using talk with her children to help them explore assumptions and pose questions—both important aspects of scientific talk. At the end of this process, Mary added the key science words *environment* and *ecosystem* to the class word wall.

Scientific inquiry: Elaboration

Scientists test their assumptions and understandings and then further elaborate on them (NRC, 2012). Mary's children returned to their small groups. She reminded them to use the scientific words they had discussed and listed on the word wall as they engaged in the next small-group activity. Mary gave each group a second mini-environment, adding cigarette butts, scraps of paper, baby food jars that contained smoky air, and baby food jars that contained dirty water to the original items. Pointing to the scientific language on the word wall, she reminded the children to use this language in their small-group discussions to (1) discuss where and how the environments or ecosystems had been damaged by humans, and (2) list the examples of damage that they considered most important in their science logs. After allowing enough time for children to discover litter and trash in the dirt, pollution in the water, and smoke in the air, Mary asked the children to reassemble on the story rug. She led a whole-class discussion about the polluted mini-environments, reminding the children to use their observational skills, science logs, and scientific vocabulary as they discussed the problems with pollution and the sources of the pollution.

Scientific inquiry: Evaluation

Once scientists have engaged in the inquiry process, they evaluate what they have learned and communicate it to others (Next Generation Science

Standards, 2011). Mary and her children used this evaluation and communication process during a debriefing period in class. With the whole group on the reading rug, Mary asked the students what they learned about their environment. As the children responded, Mary listened for the following kinds of content-related oral responses from her students: The environment is made of living (biotic) and nonliving (abiotic) things; nonliving things include soil, water, and air; and living things include plants and animals.

As they talked, Mary used their talk to analyze what they had learned, internalized, and were able to use related to the key scientific concepts in the unit. As a result, she noted that children were not referring to the ecosystem or using the language of scientists that had been introduced earlier. Thus, she asked children to look at the word wall word, identify important words that related to what they were talking about, and reviewed the definition of *ecosystem*: "the interaction of living and nonliving things in a certain area." The children then discussed how the polluted mini-environment tubs revealed what happens when humans pollute their ecosystems. As Mary led the debriefing, she used talk to label the scientific inquiry process the students had experienced, emphasizing the idea of evaluation (e.g., understanding phenomena, evaluating their understanding of phenomena, communicating their understandings).

Building on children's growing knowledge about evaluating and communicating information about phenomena, Mary asked students to create arguments supported by the evidence they had gathered and evaluated. Argumentation is an important component of the scientific inquiry process (Ehrlich & Cronin-Jones, 2013).

Engaging in scientific argumentation

Scientific argumentation involves (1) posing a question, (2) proposing a theory about the answer to the question, (3) collecting evidence pertinent to the phenomena under study to test the theory, and (4) making claims about the theory based on the evidence collected and analyzed (Ehrlich & Cronin-Jones, 2013).

A concrete example of this process occurred across several lessons when Mary read *I Took a Walk* (Cole, 1998) and gave children the opportunity to study and engage with the environmental tubs that we discussed in the previous section. At the beginning of this set of lessons, Mary and her children wondered together about the differences between living and nonliving things. They talked together in the whole group to propose a theory about the differences. Then, using scientific materials in the form of the environmental tubs, she asked the children to talk with one another so they could further develop and begin testing their theories. In this instance, children observed together using exploratory talk (Barnes, 2008). It is important to note that Mary used talk to label scientific concepts (i.e., biotic and abiotic) only after children had experienced the concepts. She did this to help them attach labels to concepts that they were coming to understand firsthand.

Coming back together as a group during the third step of the lesson, Mary and the children talked to *refine their theories* about the differences between living and nonliving things. Mary talked with children in the whole group in Step 3 to expand the process of theory building. This included adding more features to the notion of "environment." She provided scaffolded instruction (Guiding Principle 3) to steer children as they constructed broader theories now focused on how the features they had just learned are part of broader scientific concepts. During Steps 4 and 5 of the lesson, children again engaged in peer-led exploratory talk as well as whole-group scaffolded talk. This provided evidence to test their theories about living and nonliving things, environments, and ecosystems. In short, looking across Mary's sample lessons, she taught her children to *do* science by showing them ways of "talking, reasoning, observing, analyzing, and writing . . . all social processes: taught, learned, and done as members of social communities" (Lemke, 2000, p. xi).

EXAMINING CLASSROOM TALK ACROSS THE DISCIPLINES

As shown throughout these examples, talk serves different purposes and functions in different disciplines, with some mattering across disciplines. We end this chapter by identifying four key ideas about talk to consider in your own disciplinary literacy instruction.

1. *Talk is a central tool that teachers and students use to learn.* Exploratory talk can serve as a tool to understand disciplinary concepts and vocabulary. For example, in Mary's science unit, Juan and his peers helped Chris understand the difference between biotic and abiotic in their small, peer-led discussion. In Elisabeth's classroom, José didn't understand the concept of "event." Through the use of examples and non-examples, José's peers helped him to sort out this distinction.

2. *Classrooms should be engaging places where lots of meaningful, educative talk across disciplines occurs between teachers and students and between various arrangements of students (paired talk, small-group talk,*

and so forth). Both Elisabeth and Mary varied the manner in which they and their students engaged in talk. Sometimes each teacher used the IRE model of communication. However, when appropriate to their different lesson structures and formats, both teachers gave students opportunities to engage in meaningful, scaffolded exploratory talk with peers in dyads and small groups.

3. The norms for how people engage in talk vary across social and cultural groups and disciplines. In the example from Susan Philips's (1983) work with the Warm Springs Indians, there are many instances where the norms for students' talk may vary significantly from "typical" White, middle-class, mainstream norms for classroom talk. Taken together, Elisabeth and Mary have students from no less than ten different cultures. Both teachers realize that being careful to vary participation structures for talk during their lessons can likely help all students engage with and process disciplinary vocabulary, concepts, and ideas.

Disciplinary experts use talk in particular ways to convey issues and ideas. Students need to learn to use a range of discursive resources, understanding how disciplinary experts use talk as a tool to explain content. Elisabeth focused on helping her students learn to use talk to explore ideas, craft arguments using evidence, and reach consensus. Mary used talk to help her children construct and evaluate theories about the environment and ways to care for it.

4. Assessment should reflect how children use talk to construct meaning about disciplinary areas. Evaluation of student talk should focus on both content and students' ability to engage in collaborative conversations as discipline specialists (e.g., historians, scientists). Teachers should assess student knowledge and skills, as well as the opportunities they provide students to engage in substantive talk. For example, Mary provided many opportunities for her children to hear scientific talk and then to practice it among themselves in small groups and dyads. Mary continuously listened for and monitored her children's use of scientific talk, providing scaffolding when needed as her children were learning to acquire the language of science to discuss scientific concepts and processes.

PART III

Designing Your Own
Disciplinary Literacy Instruction

The third Part (Chapter 6) provides a summary of the main components of disciplinary learning and addresses ways that teachers can design disciplinary literacy instruction in their own classrooms, while ensuring that they have addressed the CCSS and the five instructional design principles we weave throughout the book. This chapter synthesizes the processes we enacted to create disciplinary literacy units and includes practical suggestions for teachers as they develop and enact their own disciplinary literacy instruction.

CHAPTER 6

Enacting Disciplinary Literacy in Elementary Classrooms

Virginia Goatley, Cynthia Brock, Catherine Weber,
Taffy Raphael, and Elisabeth Trost-Shahata

Periods of transitions can be powerful times for teachers. As the Common Core states, "The Standards define what all students are expected to know and be able to do, not how teachers should teach" (CCSS, 2010, p. 6). We can view the adoption of the Common Core as a "tipping point" (Gladwell, 2000) for renewing and revisiting our teaching. Implementing the Common Core provides an opportunity to draw on new ideas as well as established research-based practices that make sense and that improve what and how our students learn. Keep in mind that many innovations happen at the local level in schools and classrooms (Goatley & Johnston, in press), where teachers have the power to produce positive change. We invite you to join our adventure as we explore, innovate, revise, and implement new literacy and disciplinary practices in elementary classrooms.

As you implement Common Core, we encourage you to recognize and maintain best practices, yet move toward improving the needed areas it outlines. Also remember that standards, including Common Core, are simply articulated goals. Members in professional communities, formal organizations, and informal groups are the ones who must make effective decisions about how these goals can be reached, implementing policies that underlie the articulated goals.

As we noted in Chapter 1, we are at a crossroads for CCSS in terms of moving standards into highly effective curricular and instructional implementation. As professionals, we are certainly up to the task put forth in the CCSS documents: "provide students with whatever tools and knowledge their professional judgment and experience identify as most helpful for meeting the goals set out in the Standards" (2010, p. 4).

In this last chapter, we reflect on what we learned from this project and suggest how you can develop your own disciplinary literacy unit. We hope you benefit from our learning, experiences, and suggestions. First, we examine themes across Mary, Elisabeth, and Cassandra's experiences. Second, we explore what each teacher learned and plans to do to extend her own learning about disciplinary literacy. Third, we revisit the five guiding principles from Chapter 1 and use them as a framework to discuss how you can create your own disciplinary literacy unit.

DISCIPLINARY TOOLS: READING, WRITING, AND TALKING

Do you recall times that you have taught, reflected on your teaching and your students' learning, and then refined your teaching in order to teach more effectively? That is our goal in this section as we explore how Mary, Elisabeth, and Cassandra each reflected on her experience learning about disciplinary literacy, then used those reflections to improve her teaching. After discussing common themes across the three teachers' experiences, we describe each teacher's unique context and individual learning.

Common Themes

All three teachers incorporated recent research and Common Core expectations in their instruction. They also experienced both accomplishments and challenges in their teaching. An important accomplishment was increased disciplinary literacy knowledge for both the adults and children involved in the units. Not surprisingly, a common challenge for the three teachers was the need to raise expectations as to what their students might accomplish conceptually in the disciplines. Because the implementation of Common Core had just begun, many of the literacy and disciplinary concepts they taught were new to their students. All three teachers anticipate that subsequent groups of students will start the year with a stronger foundation in disciplinary literacy due to the foundation laid by teachers in earlier grade levels. For example, in contrast to today's upper elementary students, 2nd-graders in Mary's room will have a stronger foundation for the disciplines when they reach those grade levels.

Even with the intense focus on disciplinary literacy in this project, all three teachers identified the need to continue to develop their instructional practices, specifically in terms of (1) the use of resources and texts and (2) professional development. Figure 6.1 provides an overview of the teachers'

Figure 6.1. Future Instructional Plans

RESOURCES & TEXTS	PROFESSIONAL DEVELOPMENT
Use more digital resources.	Increase disciplinary content knowledge.
Use more informational and persuasive text, both in reading and writing.	Learn more about the nature of the disciplines and how disciplinary experts use reading, writing, and talking in their work. Explore how this knowledge can be translated in work with young children.
Use more texts that students can read independently and with support—in addition to whole-class read-alouds—for the development of disciplinary content.	Continue to explore how the five principles are integral to instructional decision-making processes. Consider how the five principles might be revised and/or expanded.
Use more mentor texts with the goal of helping students to become better consumers and producers of similar texts.	Maintain foundational literacy practices (such as the use of guided reading, process writing, word study, Book Club, and so on), while also increasing disciplinary literacy instruction.

future plans. It is important to remember that although the teachers are already incorporating these ideas into their instruction, they still recognize their responsibility to refine and adapt the ideas over time.

Mary's Reflections

One of the highlights of this project for Mary was working with David Crowther, a former biology teacher with expertise in science education. David helped Mary and the collaborative team to think about how scientists use talk, reading, and writing as tools to engage in the conceptual aspects of science. For example, David taught us how scientists use an *inquiry process* to engage in their work. Consistent with an inquiry approach, teachers create opportunities for children to use talk, reading, and/or writing to explore ideas and concepts. Further, science is about exploration and inquiry rather than rote memorization of decontextualized concepts. Mary's children studied environmental artifacts, talking among themselves, and taking notes in their science logs about the differences between living and nonliving things. Once her children had experiences with these concepts, Mary helped them draw on their background knowledge and new learning to attach labels to the science concepts (i.e., biotic and abiotic) they explored. Also, while engaging in the science inquiry process with her students, Mary taught them to use talk to build and evaluate theories based on evidence. Thus, not only did her students learn science terms and concepts, but *they learned to think and reason like scientists*. It is this latter point, in particular, that is important with respect to disciplinary literacy instruction.

Mary is aware that disciplinary literacy emphasizes the knowledge, skills, dispositions, and abilities used by those who work within the disciplines (Shanahan & Shanahan, 2012). Her instruction represented in this book focuses primarily on using writing (Chapter 4) and talk (Chapter 5) as tools to help her children develop disciplinary expertise in science. In future instruction, Mary plans to further emphasize how to use reading as a tool to engage in scientific inquiry. In the ideas shared in this book, Mary drew primarily on read-alouds as mentor texts to explore science concepts and writing structures. Over the next year, she will build a book library on the "taking care of the environment" theme, adding an extensive number of texts that students can read independently and that she can use during reading instruction. Mary knows that building a discipline-specific library is necessary but realizes it is not sufficient to achieve her goal of focusing on reading as a tool for disciplinary learning. She will also need to learn how scientists engage in reading and use reading within their work. Then, she will need to translate these ideas into her instruction with her 2nd-graders.

As a result of reflecting on her learning from this experience, Mary plans to ramp up her use of reading as a tool in science by tapping into her school and district professional development time as well as her professional connections. For example, Mary invited a colleague who teaches secondary science to be a part of a professional reading group of elementary colleagues who are interested in disciplinary literacy in science. The reading group will seek input from David and other science experts in the community on high-quality professional books and articles that they can read to inform their instruction. Further, they will read and discuss the recent research, such as Yopp and Yopp's (2012) article about science read-alouds to consider additional, often unaddressed, areas of science that they might explore with children. They will also collaborate together as critical colleagues while they create and implement instructional units in their respective classrooms.

Elisabeth's Reflections

After collaborating with Kathryn Obenchain and the rest of the team on this project, Elisabeth introduced more history-specific reading practices in her instruction. For example, she drew on the suggestions of Bruce VanSledright

(2002) to think explicitly about what makes reading *in* history unique *to* history. Figure 3.3 lays out VanSledright's continuum from the use of general reading practices (Levels 1 and 2) to history-specific reading practices (Levels 3 and 4) to read as historians read.

Reflecting on her learning, Elisabeth wants to further develop history-specific reading practices and resources. For example, she plans to incorporate the use of more primary sources in her instruction. Three specific resources include (1) professional journals such as the National Council for the Social Studies' *Social Studies and the Young Learner*, (2) websites such as the National Archives (http://www.archives.gov/education/research/primary-sources.html), and (3) artifacts from the local community found in museums, schools, and parks. She plans to use a broad range of sources, including documents, statues, interviews, photographs, and so forth.

Elisabeth will emphasize how to evaluate primary sources individually (Level 2 of the continuum in Figure 3.3) and read critically both within and across these sources to construct refined and evidence-based interpretations of historical events (Levels 3 and 4 of Figure 3.3). Elisabeth is aware that it will take thoughtful teaching and extensive scaffolding to help her English learners—many of whom are still in the process of acquiring English—begin to read at Levels 3 and 4 on VanSledright's continuum. One of the central goals of Level 3 is to help students look across individual sources they have analyzed at Level 2 and begin to corroborate details that inform their interpretation of a historical event. Reading at Level 4 is even more sophisticated and nuanced. At Level 4, rather than analyzing just one text for its validity, reliability, agent intentions, and so forth, the reader analyzes and critiques a set of texts related to a historical event.

Teaching toward Level 4 reading was a new concept to Elisabeth, and she recognized that none of her students engaged in Level 4 reading during the unit shared in this book. Knowing that Level 4 reading will be challenging for her students, she plans to use close reading (Beers & Probst, 2013) to help her students succeed at this level. She knows that her students will need extensive instructional scaffolding to achieve success at this complex level of historical reading.

Cassandra's Reflections

Working collaboratively with Lynda Wiest, a professor in mathematics education, helped Cassandra and the collaborative team to learn ways to use reading, writing, and talk as tools to understand mathematical concepts and ideas. For example, Lynda focused on teaching us how to communicate about, analyze, and interpret data in real-world contexts. Then, using what she learned from Lynda, Cassandra taught her students to gather, evaluate, and interpret mathematical data to use in the persuasive letters that they wrote to Governor Sandoval regarding school budget cuts.

Cassandra's teaching capitalized on recent economic events (i.e., the severe state budget cuts in Nevada in 2012). Cassandra knows that budgeting is a key conceptual aspect of mathematics instruction in 6th grade, and connecting the concept with persuasive letters led to engaging and purposeful writing for her students. Cassandra plans to expand the budget focus to explore other areas related to students' interests and the community/school context at any given time and expand beyond the topic to other areas relevant to mathematical thinking.

Although she did *begin* to help her students learn to communicate about, analyze, and interpret data in real-world settings, Cassandra feels there is much more she can do to help her students develop deeper understandings of important, real-world mathematical processes. She believes that she just started to "scratch the surface" in terms of teaching her students to use data to write persuasively. Her future plans include helping students further develop and hone their persuasive writing skills. Like Mary and Elisabeth, Cassandra meets regularly with a study group of education professionals. Consequently, she will seek her colleagues' input as she redesigns her instruction to deepen her students' understanding of how to analyze and interpret real-world data and then use those data to write more sophisticated persuasive texts.

USING THE FIVE DESIGN PRINCIPLES TO PLAN YOUR OWN UNIT

As you have seen repeatedly throughout the book, five design principles serve as a vehicle for creating and engaging in meaningful instruction. In this section, we use our own experiences with the five design principles as a framework to help you think about developing your own disciplinary literacy unit. As you read about our use of these principles, you might first revisit Chapter 1 for an overview of each principle and then consider how you can use the ideas we share to create your own disciplinary literacy unit.

Design Principle 1: Authentic Social and Cultural Practices Are Critical Features of Instructional Units

We find the four steps detailed below to be a useful and concrete way to prepare a unit with authentic cultural and social practices in mind.

Step 1. Identify a conceptual idea for the unit. Choose a disciplinary area (e.g., history, science, mathematics, literature), making sure to use the CCSS and your state resources, including standards and curriculum guides, to support grade-level expectations. Consider how you can make it relevant to your own students' cultural, linguistic, and social backgrounds. For example, Elisabeth chose to focus on Sacagawea because many of her students are immigrants or first-generation Americans. Sacagawea experienced cultural and linguistic differences as she interacted with the White settlers. Like Sacagawea, many of Elisabeth's students talked about the extensive cultural and linguistic differences they experienced as they moved from countries such as Iraq, Afghanistan, China, and so on to the United States. Cassandra chose to focus her unit on school budgets because that topic was a critical issue in her community. Local news stations, newspapers, and community members debated how to navigate the severe budget cuts at the state and local level in Nevada. These discussions occurred at the local school level as principals, teachers, and parents had to decide which teachers, materials, and programs would be eliminated from their schools.

Step 2. Consider your students' needs and your own strengths/limitations as you select materials. Think about the diversity of your students (e.g., backgrounds, interests, experiences) and the range of their learning needs. For example, Mary and Cassandra teach in different Title I schools where almost 90% of the students in their respective schools receive free and reduced lunches and approximately four-fifths of the students speak English as a second language. All of the students in Elisabeth's classroom were English learners from around the world, including India, Iraq, Ethiopia, Vietnam, Mexico, and Pakistan. Whenever possible, all three teachers get materials that are (or can be) translated into multiple languages—especially Spanish, since the majority of the English learners in all of their classrooms speak Spanish as their first language. All three teachers also seek the help of parent/community volunteers who speak English and the languages their students speak. Then classroom volunteers can help the students who are learning English understand important conceptual ideas in the students' first languages.

Consider your own background and what you bring to the disciplinary unit. For example, the three teachers featured in this book are European American women who teach students whose backgrounds differ in terms of home languages spoken, ethnicity, and economic levels. Mary, Elisabeth, and Cassandra are all familiar with the work of Susan Philips (1983) and

Kathryn Au (1980) that we shared in Chapter 5. As one example, Philips's work illustrated how Indian children on the Warm Springs Reservation used talk differently as compared with their European American teachers. Au's work illustrated how Native Hawaiian children were more successful when their teachers used "talk story"—a style of discourse with which the children were familiar—during literacy instruction. Mary, Elisabeth, and Cassandra are aware that because their cultural and linguistic backgrounds differ from those of most of their students, there may be cultural mismatches between their use of talk, reading, and writing and their students' use of talk, reading, and writing. So, they honor and start with their students' cultural and linguistic norms as they plan their instruction. Then, they provide scaffolding to move from students' knowledge and experiences to provide meaningful disciplinary literacy instruction in terms of talk, reading, and writing (Freire, 2005).

Step 3. Find friends and colleagues at your own school and in other schools who want to collaborate with you. It is incredibly helpful to collaborate with same grade-level peers to build resources for shared units. In our own experience, collaborative communities are the foundation on which any policy can be integrated into ongoing professional change (Goatley, 2009; Goatley, Highfield, Bentley, Pardo, Folkert, Scherer, Raphael, & Grattan, 1994; Raphael, Florio-Ruane, George, Hasty, & Highfield, 2004). If your school does not have such a community, there are many online options such as NCTE's Connected Community (http://www.ncte.org/community) and the NCLE Literacy in Learning Exchange (http://www.literacyinlearningex change.org/).

Step 4. Develop a staircase curriculum at your school. One long-standing criticism of teacher preparation is that elementary teachers do not have the content knowledge needed to successfully teach the disciplines (Shulman, 1987). Creating a staircase curriculum (Au & Raphael, 2011) within schools helps foster meaningful conversations about what to teach to support disciplinary learning across the grade levels. Through such conversations, you can become an expert on the content required at your grade level, but also collaborate with peers to understand and anticipate what children learn in the grade levels before and after yours. With your grade-level peers, read and share professional books, content books (e.g., an informational text on budgeting), professional journal articles, and so forth to increase your content knowledge about grade-specific disciplinary concepts.

Design Principle 2: An Optimal Learning Model
Provides a Framework for Instruction

The two steps detailed below are useful in incorporating an optimal learning model.

Step 1. Consider your disciplinary literacy instructional goals. Think about the scaffolding your own students will need to use reading, writing, and talking as tools for disciplinary learning. Ask yourself what instructional supports you need to provide for your students to help them reach the set goals. Questions to ask yourself include: What background knowledge, skills, and dispositions do my students bring to the study of each discipline? How can I build on my students' backgrounds in my instructional planning to reach my instructional goals? For example, the teachers featured in this book attended carefully to the nature of scaffolding that their students needed during their disciplinary literacy instruction, as seen in each classroom example throughout the book.

Consider the different types of scaffolding that are required for the various disciplines. For example, Elisabeth knows that disciplinary reading instruction in history requires complex practices such as evaluating multiple sources and then piecing together insights across sources to develop understandings of historical events. She knows that she will need to provide effective scaffolding to her English learners to reach these high levels of disciplinary understanding. Further, she knows that some students bring preconceived notions about historical and current events that may not be historically accurate or they may have only minimal background knowledge about key U.S. events and issues. Scaffolding for lessons in mathematical and scientific thinking will differ from those in history.

Step 2. Select one discipline as a focus area to begin exploring and planning disciplinary instruction. Within the focus discipline you choose, start small. Trying to do everything at once can be frustrating and overwhelming for you and your students. Rather than trying to focus on reading, writing, and talking all at once, we recommend choosing one tool (i.e., reading, writing, or talking) as a starting point. From there, you can bring in the other tools and extend your units to include other disciplines. For example, Elisabeth knows that teaching her students to read like historians is a very complex undertaking. In the next iteration of her unit, she will focus primarily on helping her students learn to read like historians. She will add writing and talking like historians to later iterations of the unit.

Develop one unit, try it out, and tweak it to make it better each time. Then, try developing another unit drawing on what you learned. As we mentioned in the previous section of this chapter, this is exactly what Mary, Elisabeth, and Cassandra did.

Design Principle 3: Key Inquiry Questions Give Structure to Disciplinary Study

These two steps are helpful in creating strong questions that give your study its structure.

Step 1. Start with disciplinary standards, as well as Common Core, to match grade-level goals of a particular subject as you develop your own inquiry questions. Make sure you know how the local and state standards provide an outline for the curriculum in your school district. Be sure to collaborate with your peers to encourage a staircase curriculum, yet avoid complete duplication of similar conceptual ideas. Ask yourself the following question: How can I design a key inquiry question that will be motivating and engaging to my students and address disciplinary standards as well as the CCSS? For example, each teacher in this book focused on a central inquiry question, rather than a topic. Mary asked: How do we care for our soil, land, and water? Elisabeth asked: Why do we remember Sacagawea? Cassandra asked: How do we make decisions about educational budgets and budgeting in our school district and our school? As each teacher developed and refined her inquiry, she also referred to the CCSS and the disciplinary standards that related to her inquiry focus.

Avoid selecting narrow topics with little substance. Make sure to design your disciplinary literacy unit around a theme, major conceptual idea, or central inquiry question rather than simply a topic. For example, all three teachers in this book started with powerful, rigorous conceptual ideas. They also designed guiding inquiry questions that their students found motivating and compelling.

Step 2. Realize that it can take time and effort to develop a high-quality inquiry question/focus. Mary, Elisabeth, and Cassandra all worked hard to develop meaningful focus questions for their units. They spent time revising and refining their questions. They found it helpful to get feedback from colleagues as they were in the process of refining their focus questions for their units. To continually build up a professional set of books, primary sources, instructional examples, and so forth is a long-term goal, especially relative to keeping the unit current and engaging.

Design Principle 4: Composing Meaning Within and Across Units Requires a Range of Resources (Including Both Conventional Texts and Digital Media)

The two steps that guide enacting this principle focus on aspects of gathering and organizing resources.

Step 1. Consider the resources you have available as you begin planning instruction for your disciplinary unit. Think about what other resources you may be able to access for free from local libraries, museums, or the Internet. What resources do you have and what resources will you need to collect? Do an analysis of the resources you have and how you will use them for instruction. Think about the following questions: What texts do I have that are related to the theme that might be useful for independent and instructional reading as well as read-alouds? How might I use artifacts, primary sources, graphs, comics, interviews, or other mentor texts to support instruction? For example, Mary, Elisabeth, and Cassandra used a range of texts (for read-aloud and guided instruction) and resources throughout their units.

As you develop your own disciplinary literacy units, we suggest that you consider the range of texts your students will read, the manner in which they will engage in the writing process, and the kinds of writing they will produce. Capitalize on students' interests by engaging them in the process of building your resource library. Ask them what they would like to explore further and have them make suggestions about additions to the classroom library.

Step 2. Continually build your resource library by adding new materials and rotating out those that may not be as effective for instruction. Do you have really old books in your classroom library? Request school funds to purchase trade books after a careful critique of their accuracy and text level. Use the trade book suggestions from the professional organizations to help you preview possible texts for each unit. Be careful to select across a range of text difficulty and type of text. Primary sources are often free and add substantial content opportunities that will be engaging to students.

Design Principle 5: Authentic Assessments Must Reflect the Different Types of Meaning-Making Processes Students Use as They Read, Write, and Talk in the Course of Instruction

The three steps for Principle 5 focus on your goals, plans, and existing assessment structures.

Step 1. As you create an assessment system in your own classroom, consider your instructional goals as well as your goals for gathering information. Think about your instructional goals for your students' learning. What do you already know about them? What do you need to know to plan targeted instruction? The teachers in this book understand the importance of both daily and long-term assessments in order to plan effective instruction to meet the specific needs of the students in their classrooms. For example, Elisabeth assessed students' prior knowledge about history content before engaging students in the unit of study. This enabled her to help her students build background knowledge and make learning more meaningful and effective.

Consider what tools you will use to gather information. When will you gather information (e.g., before, during, after instruction) and how frequently (e.g., daily, weekly, monthly, yearly)? Also, think about how you will use the information to plan for instruction and differentiate instruction to meet all students' needs.

Step 2. Create a plan for assessing all aspects of literacy learning (e.g., reading, writing, talk) strategically and systematically. If you teach an idea, there should be a way of assessing whether students have learned it. View assessment as an ongoing process of information gathering to inform instruction (day-to-day and throughout a unit/semester/year), rather than as an isolated event that happens after instruction.

Include yourself in your assessment plans. In addition to measuring students' progress, evaluate your own growth over time. Think about the learning opportunities you provide your students and the effectiveness of your instruction.

Step 3. Think about what structures you already have in place in your classroom and analyze the effectiveness of your current assessment system. What areas of literacy instruction are you assessing effectively? What areas are not being assessed or could use improvement? What changes do you need to make to your assessment system to ensure that you have the information you need about students' abilities and progress over time, as well as your own development?

Assessing throughout the daily schedule (e.g., literacy time, science, math) allows you to gain a deeper understanding of what students know and are able to do, making it possible to plan strategically.

CONCLUDING COMMENTS

As we conclude this book, the following key assertions likely sound familiar. They are critical to successfully using literacy as a tool for disciplinary teaching.

1. *The "Why" of Disciplinary Literacy:* The disciplines need to be at the forefront of instruction, not relegated to a simple notion of incorporating the content via literacy instruction.
2. *The "What" of Disciplinary Literacy:* Although there are overlapping features across the disciplines, each discipline has its own unique content, norms, and vocabulary. Reading, writing, and talking are tools for disciplinary learning. Students need to learn the content, norms, and vocabulary within and across disciplines.
3. *The "How" of Disciplinary Literacy:* Children need to learn to read and write a wide variety of genres and forms for different purposes and audiences. When we are meaningfully teaching the disciplines, educators need to know about this range of genres, forms, audiences, and purposes, and they need to know how to teach across this range of forms and purposes. For example, students need to learn to use science notebooks, primary sources, and to read and write persuasive texts. Teachers also need to teach students how to use reading, writing, and talk as tools in a variety of forms based on purpose and audience.

Children's Literature

Adler, D. A. (2003). *A picture book of Lewis and Clark*. New York: Holiday House.

Braun, S. (2009). *On our way home*. New York: Boxer Books/Sterling Publishing.

Cannon, J. (1993). *Stellaluna*. Orlando, FL: Harcourt Books.

Cole, H. (1998). *I took a walk*. New York, NY: Greenwillow Books.

Corral, K., & Corral, H. (1995). *My Denali: Exploring Alaska's favorite national park with Hannah Corral*. Seattle, WA: Alaska Northwest Books.

Fradin, J. B., & Fradin, D. B. (2002). *Who was Sacagawea?* New York, NY: Grosset & Dunlap.

Muth, J. J. (2002). *The three questions*. New York, NY: Scholastic.

Rowland, D. (1989). *The story of Sacagawea, guide to Lewis and Clark*. New York, NY: Bantam Doubleday Dell Books for Young Readers.

Schieszka, J. (1989). *The true story of the three little pigs*. New York: Puffin Books.

Seeger, L. V. (2010). *What if?* New York, NY: Roaring Brook Press.

Weber, S. (2005). *Two in the wilderness: Adventures of a mother and daughter in the Adirondack mountains*. Honesdale, PA: Calkins Creek Books.

Williams, B. (1998). *Your environment: Geography starts here*. Raintree.

References

Allen, C. A. (2001). *The multigenre research paper: Voice, passion, and discovery in grades 4–6.* Westport, CT: Heinemann.

Allington R, & Gabriel, R. (2012). Every child, every day. *Educational Leadership, 69*(6), 10–15.

Alvermann, D. E., & Swafford, J. (1989). Do content area strategies have a research base? *Journal of Reading, 32*(5), 388–394.

Anders, P. L., & Guzetti, B. J. (1996). *Literacy instruction in the content areas.* Orlando, FL: Harcourt, Brace, & Company.

Au, K. H. (1980). Participation structures in a reading lesson with Hawaiian children: Finding a culturally appropriate instructional event. *Anthropology and Education Quarterly, 11*, 91–115.

Au, K. H., & Raphael, T. E. (1998). Curriculum and teaching in literature-based programs. In T. E. Raphael & K. H. Au (Eds.), *Literature-based instruction: Reshaping the curriculum* (pp. 123–148). Norwood, MA: Christopher-Gordon Publishers.

Au, K. H., & Raphael, T. E. (2011). The staircase curriculum: Whole-school collaboration to improve literacy achievement. *The NERA Journal, 46*(2), 1–8.

Barab, S. A., Gresalfi, M., Dodge, T., & Ingram-Goble, A. (2010). Narratizing disciplines and disciplinizing narratives: Games as 21st century curriculum. *International Journal of Gaming and Computer-Mediated Simulations, 2*(1), 17–30.

Barnes, D. (2008). Exploratory talk for learning. In N. Mercer & S. Hodgkinson (Eds.), *Exploring talk in school* (pp. 1–16). London: Sage Publications.

Barnes, M. K., Johnson, E., & Neff, L. (2010). Learning through process drama in the first grade. *Social Studies and the Young Learner, 22*(4), 19–24.

Bear, D. R., Invernizzi, M. R., Templeton, S., & Johnston, F. R. (2011). *Words their way: Word study for phonics, vocabulary, and spelling instruction.* London: Pearson.

Beauchamp, A., Kusnick, J., & McCallum, R. (2011). *Success in science through dialogue, reading, and writing.* Davis, CA: Sacramento Area Science Project.

Beddow, M. (2012). Dear Cesar Chavez: Writing persuasive letters in the sixth grade. *Social Studies and the Young Learner, 24*(3), 11–12.

Beers, K., & Probst, R. E. (2013). *Notice and note: Strategies for close reading.* Portsmouth, NH: Heinemann.

Benjamin, A. (2011). *Math in plain English: Literacy strategies for the mathematics classroom.* New York, NY: Routledge.

Berson, I. R. (2009). Here's what we have to say! Podcasting in the early childhood classroom. *Social Studies and the Young Learner, 21*(4), 8–11.

Boyd, F. (2012/2013, December/January). The Common Core State Standards and diversity: Unpacking the text exemplars presented in appendix B. *Reading Today, 30*(3), 10–11.

Boyd, M., & Galda, L. (2011). *Real talk in elementary classrooms: Effective oral language practice.* New York, NY: Guilford.

Brock, C. H. (2007). Exploring an English learner's literacy learning opportunities: A collaborative case study analysis. *Urban Education, 42*(5), 470–501.

Brock, C. H., & Raphael, T. E. (2005). *Windows to language, literacy, and culture: Insights from an English-language learner.* Newark, DE: The International Reading Association.

Brophy, J., & Alleman, J. (2006). *Children's thinking about cultural universals.* Mahwah, NJ: Erlbaum.

Burke, A. (2011). National day of listening comes to Midland, Michigan: A StoryCorps Project. *Social Studies & The Young Learner, 24*(2), 5–8.

Burton, M., & Mims, P. (2012). Calculating puddle size. *Teaching Children Mathematics, 18*(8), 474–480.

Calkins, L., Ehrenworth, M., & Lehman, C. (2012). *Pathways to the Common Core: Accelerating achievement.* Portsmouth, NH: Heinemann.

Cazden, C. (2001). *Classroom discourse: The language of teaching and learning* (2nd ed.). Portsmouth, NH: Heinemann.

Clay, M. M. (1993). *Reading Recovery: A guidebook for teachers in training.* Portsmouth, NH: Heinemann.

Coiro, J. (2003). Rethinking comprehension strategies to better prepare students for critically evaluating content on the Internet. *The NERA Journal, 39*, 29–34.

Coiro, J. (2011). Talking about reading as thinking: Models of hidden complexities of online reading comprehension. *Theory Into Practice, 50*, 107–115.

Coiro, J., & Dobler, E. (2007). Exploring the online reading comprehension strategies used by sixth-grade skilled readers to search for and locate information on the Internet. *Reading Research Quarterly, 42*(2), 214–257.

Coleman, D., & Pimentel, S. (2012). *Revised publisher's criteria for the Common Core State Standards.* Retrieved from http://groups.ascd.org/resource/documents/122463-PublishersCriteriaforLiteracyforGrades3-12.pdf

Common Core State Standards Initiative. (2010). *Common Core State Standards for English language arts & literacy in history/social studies, science, and technical subjects.* Retrieved from http://www.corestandards.org/the-standards

Cooperative Children's Book Center. (2013). *Choices* essays on publishing trends. Retrieved from http://www.education.wisc.edu/ccbc/books/choices.asp#observ

Cross, D. I. (2009). Creating optimal mathematics learning environments: Combining argumentation and writing to enhance achievement. *International Journal of Science & Mathematics Education, 7*(5), 905–930.

Culham, R. (2003). *6+1 Traits of writing: The complete guide grades 3 and up.* New York: Scholastic Professional Books.

Derewianka, B., & Jones, P. (2012). *Teaching language in context.* Melbourne, Australia: Oxford University Press.

Draper, R. J. (2008). Redefining content area literacy teacher education: Finding my voice through collaboration. *Harvard Educational Review, 78*(1), 60–83.

Duke, N. K. (2000). 3.6 minutes per day: The scarcity of informational texts in first grade. *Reading Research Quarterly, 35*, 202–224.

Duke, N. K. (2004). The case for informational text. *Educational Leadership, 61*(6), 40–44.

Duke, N. K., & Carlisle, J. (2010). The development of comprehension. In M. L. Kamil, P. D. Pearson, E. B. Moje, & P. P. Afflerbach (Eds.), *Handbook of reading research, Volume IV* (pp. 199–228). New York, NY: Routledge.

Duke, N. K., Caughlan, S., Juzwik, M. M., & Martin, N. M. (2012). Teaching genre with purpose. *Educational Leadership, 69*(6), 34–39.

Dutton, D. (1987). Why intentionalism won't go away. In A. J. Cascardi (Ed.), *Literature and the question of philosophy* (pp. 1–17). Baltimore, MD: Johns Hopkins University Press.

Dyson, A. H. (2003). *The brothers and sisters learn to write: Popular literacies in childhood and school cultures.* New York, NY: Teachers College Press.

Ebbers, M. (2002). Science text sets: Using various genres to promote literacy and inquiry. *Language Arts, 80*(1), 40-50.

Eeds, M., & Wells, D. (1989). Grand conversations: An exploration of meaning construction in literature discussion groups. *Research in the Teaching of English, 23*(1), 4–29.

Ehrlich, R., & Cronin-Jones, L. (2013, Summer). Hook, line, and sinker: Using a global fisheries role-play to enhance students' scientific discourse and argumentation skills. *The Science Teacher*, 57–61.

Elbow, P. (1998). *Writing without teachers.* New York: Oxford University Press.

Fang, Z., & Schleppegrell, M. J. (2010). Disciplinary literacies across content areas: Supporting secondary reading through functional language analysis. *Journal of Adolescent and Adult Literacy, 53*(7), 587–597.

Fish, S. (1982). *Is there a text in this class? The authority of interpretive communities.* Cambridge, MA: Harvard University Press.

Fisher, D., & Frey, N. (2012). Close reading in elementary schools. *The Reading Teacher, 66*(3), 179–188.

Fisher, D., Frey, N., & Lapp, D. (2012). *Text complexity: Raising rigor in reading.* Newark, DE: International Reading Association.

Florio-Ruane, S., & Raphael, T. E. (2004). Reconsidering our research: Collaboration, complexity, design, and the problem of "scaling up what works." *National Reading Conference Yearbook, 54,* 170–189.

Fountas, I. C. & Pinnell, G. S. (1996). *Guided reading: Good first teaching for all children.* Portsmouth, NH: Heinemann.

Fountas, I. C., & Pinnell, G. S. (2006). *Teaching for comprehension and fluency: Thinking, talking, and writing about reading, K–8.* Portsmouth, NH: Heinemann.

Fradin, J., & Fradin, D. (2002). *Who was Sacagawea?* New York: Grossett & Dunlap.

Freire, P. (2005). *Pedagogy of the oppressed (30th anniversary edition).* New York: Continuum.

Gallagher, S., & Hodges, S. (2010). Let's teach students to prioritize: Reconsidering "wants" and "needs." *Social Studies and the Young Learner, 22*(3), 14–16.

Gallas, K. (1995). *Talking their way into science: Hearing children's questions and theories, responding with curricula.* New York, NY: Teachers College Press.

Gavelek, J. R., & Raphael, T. E. (1996). Changing talk about text: New roles for teachers and students. *Language Arts, 73*(3), 182–192.

Gavelek, J. R., Raphael, T. E., Biondo, S. E., & Wang, D. (2000). Integrated literacy instruction. In M. L. Kamil, P. B. Mosenthal, P. D. Pearson, & R. Barr (Eds.), *Handbook of reading research: Volume III* (pp. 587–608). Mahwah, NJ: Erlbaum.

Gee, J. (2012). *Social linguistics and literacies: Ideologies in discourses* (4th ed.). New York, NY: Routledge.

Gladwell, M. (2000). *The tipping point: How little things can make a difference.* Boston, MA: Little Brown.

Goatley, V. J. (2009). Thinking together: Creating and sustaining professional learning communities. In C. A. Lassonde & S. E. Israel (Eds.), *Teacher collaboration for professional learning: Facilitating study, research, and inquiry communities* (pp. 143–144). San Francisco, CA: Jossey-Bass.

Goatley, V. J. (2011, August/September). Finding a voice in professional literacy communities. *Reading Today, 29*(1), 16–17.

Goatley, V. J. (2012). Slicing and dicing the ELA Common Core Standards. *Principal, 92*(1), 16–21.

Goatley, V. J., Brock, C., & Raphael, T. E. (1995). Diverse learners participating in regular education "book clubs." *Reading Research Quarterly, 30*(3), 353–380.

Goatley, V. J., Highfield, K. A, Bentley, J., Pardo, L. S., Folkert, J., Scherer, P., Raphael, T. E., & Grattan, K. (1994). Empowering teachers to be researchers: A collaborative approach. *The Teacher Research Journal: A Journal of Classroom Inquiry, 1*(2), 128–144.

Goatley, V. J., & Johnston, P. (in press). Innovation, research, and policy in the evolution of classroom teaching. *Language Arts.*

Goatley, V. J., & Overturf, B. (2011). *Common Core: Seven opportunities to transform English language arts curriculum.* Retrieved from http://www.edutopia.org/blog/common-core-state-standards-2-virginia-goatley

Gomez, D. (2010). Let's go to market! Field trips to discover economics and culture. *Social Studies and the Young Learner, 22*(3), 21–24.

Graves, D. H. (1983). *Writing: Teachers and children at work.* Exeter, NH: Heinemann Educational Books.

Graves, D. H., & Hansen, J. (1983). The author's chair. *Language Arts, 60*, 176–183.

Greenleaf, C., Cribb, G., Howlett, H., & Moore, D. (2010). Inviting outsiders inside disciplinary literacies: An interview with Cynthia Greenleaf, Gayle Cribb, and Heather Howlett. *Journal of Adolescent and Adult Literacy, 54*(4), 291–293.

Greenleaf, C., Schoenbach, R., & Cziko, C. (2001). Apprenticing adolescent readers to academic literacy. *American Educational Research Journal, 71*(1), 79–129.

Guthrie, J. T., Coddington, C. S., & Wigfield, A. (2009). Profiles of motivation for reading among African American and Caucasian students. *Journal of Literacy Research, 41*, 317–353.

Guthrie, J. T., & Klauda, S. L. (2012). Making textbook reading meaningful. *Educational Leadership, 69*(6), 64–68.

Guthrie, J. T., Wigfield, A., & Humenick, N. M. (2006). Influences of stimulating tasks on reading motivation and comprehension. *Journal of Educational Research, 99*(4), 232–245.

Gutiérrez, K. (2008). Developing a sociocritical literacy in the third space. *Reading Research Quarterly, 43*(2), 148–164.

Hansen, J. (1983). Authors respond to authors. *Language Arts, 60*(8), 970–976.

Henry, L. A. (2006). SEARCHing for an answer: The critical role of new literacies while reading on the Internet. *The Reading Teacher, 59*(7), 614–627.

Herber, H. L. (1970). *Teaching reading in content areas.* Englewood Cliffs, NJ: Prentice-Hall.

Herman, P., & Wardrip, P. (2012). Reading to learn: Helping students comprehend readings in science class. *Science Teacher, 48*–51.

Hiebert, E. H. (2012). Seven actions that teachers can take right now. Text Project & The University of California, Santa Cruz. Retrieved from http://textproject.org/professional-development/text-matters/7-actions-that-teachers-can-take-right-now-text-complexity/

Hiebert, E. H., & Sailors, M. (2009). *Finding the right texts: What works for beginning and struggling readers.* New York, NY: Guilford.

Hoyt, L., & Boswell, K. (2012). *Crafting nonfiction intermediate: Lessons on writing process, traits, and craft.* Portsmouth, NH: Heinemann.

International Society for Technology in Education (ISTE). (2007). *National Educational Technology Standards.* Retrieved from: http://www.iste.org/standards

Jenks, C. E. (2010). Using oral history in the elementary school classroom. *Social Studies & The Young Learner, 23*(1), 31–32.

Jeong, J. S., Gaffney, J. S., & Choi, J. O. (2010). Availability and use of informational text in second, third, and fourth grades. *Research in the Teaching of English, 44*, 435–456.

Johnston, P. (2004). *Choice words: How our language affects children's learning.* Portland, ME: Stenhouse.

Judy, S. N. (1974). *Explorations in the teaching of secondary English: A source book for experiential teaching.* New York, NY: Dodd, Mead & Company.

Kamberelis, G. (1998). Relations between children's literacy diets and genre development: You write what you read. *Literacy Teaching and Learning, 3*(1), 7–53.

Kinniburgh, L. H., & Busby, R. S. (2008). No social studies left behind: Integrating social studies during the elementary literacy block. *Journal of Content Area Reading, 7*(1), 55–85.

Kucan, L., & Palincsar, A. S. (2013). *Comprehension instruction through text-based discussion.* Newark, DE: International Reading Association.

Larson, L. C. (2009). Reader Response meets New Literacies: Empowering readers in online learning communities. *The Reading Teacher, 62*, 638–648.

Lemke, J. (2000). *Talking science: Language, learning and values.* Norwood, NJ: Ablex Publishing.

Leu, D. J., Kinzer, C. K., Coiro, J. L., & Cammack, D. W. (2004). Toward a theory of new literacies emerging from the Internet and other information and communication technologies. In R. B. Ruddell & N. J. Unrau (Eds.), *Theoretical models and processes of reading* (5th ed., pp. 1570–1615). Newark, DE: IRA.

Levstik, L., & Barton, K. (2010). *Doing history: Investigating with children in elementary and middle schools.* New York, NY: Routledge.

Linder, C. (2011). *Exploring the landscape of scientific literacy.* New York, NY: Routledge, Taylor & Francis Group.

Lindfors, J. W. (2008). *Children's talk: Connecting reading, writing, and talk.* New York, NY: Teachers College Press.

Lipson, M. Y., Valencia, S. W., Wixson, K. K., & Peters, C. W. (1993). Integration and thematic teaching: Integration to improve teaching and learning. *Language Arts, 70*(4), 252–363.

Llewellyn, D. (2013). Making and defending/scientific arguments: Strategies that prepare your students for the new wave of curriculum reform. *Science Teacher, 80*(5), 33–38.

Loveless, T. (2012). How well are American students learning? With sections on predicting the effect of the Common Core State Standards, achievement gaps on the two NAEP tests, and misinterpreting international test scores (The Brown Center on Educational Policy, Trans.). Retrieved from: http://www.brookings.edu/~/media/newsletters/0216_brown_education_loveless.pdf

Maloch, B., & Bomer, R. (2013). Teaching about and with informational texts: What does research teach us? *Language Arts, 90*(6), 441–450.

Marinak, B. A., & Gambrell, L. B. (2009). Ways to teach about informational text. *Social Studies and the Young Learner, 22*(1), 19–22.

Matz Rosen, L. (1992). Afloat on a sea of talk. *Language Arts Journal of Michigan: 8*(1), Article 2. Retrieved from http://dx.doi.org/10.9707/2168-149X.1618

Metz, S. (2012). Reading, writing, and science. *Science Teacher, 79*(1), 6.

Metz, S. (2013). Let's argue! *Science Teacher, 80*, 6.

Miller, J. E. (2010). Quantitative literacy across the curriculum: Integrating skills from English composition, mathematics, and substantive disciplines. *The Educational Forum, 74*, 334–346.

Mohr, K. (2006). Children's choices for recreational reading: A three-part investigation of selection preferences, rationales, and processes. *Journal of Literacy Research, 38*(1), 81–104.

Moje, E. B. (2007). Developing socially just subject matter instruction: A review of the literature on disciplinary literacy. In L. Parker (Ed.), *Review of research in education* (pp. 1–44). Washington, DC: American Educational Research Association.

Moje, E. B. (2008). Foregrounding the disciplines in secondary literacy teaching and learning: A call for change. *Journal of Adolescent & Adult Literacy, 52*(2), 96–107.

Moje, E. B. (2010). Comprehension in the subject areas: The challenges of comprehension, grades 7–12, and what to do about them. In K. Ganske & D. Fisher (Eds.), *Comprehension across the curriculum: Perspectives and practices K–12.* New York, NY: Guilford.

Moje, E. B., Stockdill, D., Kim, K., & Kim, H. (2010). The role of text in disciplinary learning. In M. L. Kamil, P. D. Pearson, E. B. Moje, & P. P. Afflerbach (Eds.), *Handbook of reading research* (Vol. IV, pp. 453–486). New York, NY: Routledge.

National Archives. (2013). *Finding primary sources.* Retrieved from http://www.archives.gov/education/research/primary-sources.html

National Center for Literacy Education. (2013). *Literacy in learning exchange.* Retrieved from http://www.literacyinlearningexchange.org/

National Council for the Social Studies. (2013). *Notable tradebooks for young people.* Retrieved from: http://www.socialstudies.org/resources/notable

National Council of Teachers of English. (2011). *Literacies of disciplines: A policy research brief.* Retrieved from http://www.ncte.org/library/NCTEFiles/Resources/Journals/CC/0211-sep2011/CC0211Policy.pdf

National Council of Teachers of English. (2013). *Chat with others on the NCTE connected community*. Retrieved from http://www.ncte.org/community

National Institute of Child Health and Human Development. (2000). *Report of the National Reading Panel. Teaching children to read: An evidence-based assessment of the scientific research literature on reading and its implications for reading instruction* (NIH Publication No. 00-4769). Washington, DC: U.S. Government Printing Office.

National Research Council. (2012). *A framework for K–12 science education: Practices, crosscutting concepts, and core ideas*. Washington, DC: National Academics Press.

National Science Teachers Association. (2013). *Outstanding science tradebooks for students K–12*. Retrived from: http://www.nsta.org/publications/ostb/

Neuman, S. B., & Gambrell, L. B. (2013). *Quality reading instruction in the age of the Common Core standards*. Newark, DE: International Reading Association.

New York State Education Department. (2010, June 22). *Board of Regents approves assessment cost reductions*. Retrieved from http://www.oms.nysed.gov/press/AssessmentCostReductions.html

Next Generations Science Standards Lead States. (2011). *Next generation science standards: For states, by states*. Washington, DC: National Academies Press. Retrieved from http://www.nap.edu/NGSS/

Nitko, A. J. (1996). *Educational assessment of students* (3rd ed.). Des Moines, IA: Prentice-Hall.

Nussbaum, E. (2002). Scaffolding argumentation in the social studies classroom. *Social Studies, 93*(2), 79–83.

Ogle, D. (1986). K-W-L: A teaching model that develops active reading of an expository text. *The Reading Teacher, 39*, 564–570.

Ogle, D., Klemp, R., & McBride, B. (2007). *Building literacy in social studies: Strategies for improving comprehension and critical thinking*. Alexandria, VA: ASCD.

Opitz, M. (1998). Text sets: One way to flex your grouping—in 1st grade too! *The Reading Teacher, 51*(7), 622–624.

Ozgungor, S., & Guthrie, J. T. (2004). Interactions among elaborative interrogation, knowledge, and interest in the process of constructing knowledge from text. *Journal of Educational Psychology, 96*, 437–443.

Pace, J. (2007, December 19). Why we need to save (and strengthen) social studies. *Education Week, 27*(16), 17–26. Retrieved from http://www.edweek.org/ew/articles/2007/12/19/16pace.h27.html

Palincsar, A. S., & Brown, A. L. (1984). Reciprocal teaching of comprehension-fostering and comprehension-monitoring activities. *Cognition and Instruction, 1*(2), 117–175.

Pappas, C. (2006). The information book genre: Its role in integrated science literacy research and practice. *Reading Research Quarterly, 41,* 226–250.

Parker, W., & Hess, D. (2001). Teaching with and for discussion. *Teaching and Teacher Education, 17,* 273–289.

Pearson, P. D. (1986). Twenty years of research in reading comprehension. In T. E. Raphael (Ed.), *Contexts for school-based literacy* (pp. 43–62). New York, NY: Random House.

Pearson, P. D. (2012, March 9). No Child Left Behind's effect on literacy. *Washington Post.* Retrieved from http://www.washingtonpost.com/blogs/answer-sheet/post/no-child-left-behinds-effect-on-literacy/2012/03/08/gIQAPohO0R_blog.html?wprss=rss_answer-sheet

Pearson, P. D. (2013). Research foundations of the Common Core standards in English language arts. In S. B. Neuman & L. B. Gambrell (Eds.), *Quality reading instruction in the age of the Common Core standards.* Newark, DE: International Reading Association.

Philips, S. (1983). *The invisible culture: Communication in classroom and community on the Warm Springs Indian Reservation.* Long Grove, IL: Waveland Press.

Potter, L. A. (2009). Teaching with documents, and documents, and more documents: The National Archives Digital Partnerships. *Social Education, 73*(3), 109–112.

Powell, R., & Davidson, N. (2005). The donut house: Real world literacy in an urban kindergarten classroom. *Language Arts, 82*(5), 248–256.

Purcell-Gates, V., Duke, N., & Martineau, J. (2007). Learning to read and write genre-specific text: Roles of authentic experience and explicit teaching. *Reading Research Quarterly, 42,* 8–45.

Raphael, T. E., Florio-Ruane, S., & George, M. (2001). Book Club Plus: A conceptual framework to organize literacy instruction. *Language Arts, 79*(2), 159–168.

Raphael, T. E., Florio-Ruane, S., George, M. A., Hasty, N. L., & Highfield, K. (2004). *Book Club Plus: A literacy framework for primary grades.* Littleton, MA: Small Planet Communications, Inc.

Raphael, T. E., & McMahon, S. I. (1994). Book Club: An alternative framework for reading instruction. *The Reading Teacher, 48*(2), 102–116.

Raphael, T. E., Pardo, L., & Highfield, K. (2002). *Book Club: A literature-based curriculum.* Lawrence, MA: Small Planet Communications.

Redford, C. B. (2011). Celebrate mathematical curiosity. *Teaching children mathematics, 18*(2), 144–151.

Risinger, C. F. (2010). Using online field trips and tours in social studies. *Social Education, 74*(3), 137–138.

Romano, T. (2000). *Blending genre, altering style.* Portsmouth, NH: Boynton/Cook.

Rosenblatt, L. (1938). *Literature as exploration.* New York: Appleton-Century.

Rosenblatt, L. (2005). *Making meaning with texts: Selected essays*. Portsmouth, NH: Heinemann.

Routman, R. (2003). *Reading essentials: The specifics you need to teach reading well*. Portsmouth, NH: Heinemann.

Routman, R. (2004). *Writing essentials: Raising expectations and results while simplifying teaching*. Portsmouth, NH: Heinemann.

Sampson, V., Enderle, P., & Grooms, J. (2013). Argumentation in science education: Helping students understand the nature of scientific argumentation so they can meet the new science standards. *Science Teacher, 80*(5), 30–33.

Scanlon, D., Anderson, K., & Sweeney, J. (2010). *Early intervention for reading difficulties: The interactive strategies approach*. New York, NY: Guilford.

Scribner, S., & Cole, M. (1981). *The psychology of literacy*. Cambridge, MA: Harvard University Press.

Seixas, P. (1993). Historical understanding among adolescents in a multicultural setting. *Curriculum Inquiry 23*(3), 301–327.

Shanahan, T., & Shanahan, C. (2008). Teaching disciplinary literacy to adolescents: Rethinking content-area literacy. *Harvard Educational Review, 78*, 40–59.

Shanahan, T., & Shanahan, C. (2012). What is disciplinary literacy and why does it matter? *Topics in Language Disorders, 32*, 1–12.

Shulman, L. (1986). Those who understand: Knowledge growth in teaching. *Educational Researcher, 15*(2), 4–14.

Sims Bishop, R. (2011). *Diversity in children's literature: What does it matter in today's educational climate*. A paper presented at the National Council of Teachers of English, Chicago.

Snow, C., Griffin, P., & Burns, M. S. (2005). *Knowledge to support the teaching of reading: Preparing teachers for a changing world*. San Francisco, CA: Jossey-Bass.

Soter, A. O., Wilkinson, I. A., Murphy, P. K., Rudge, L., Reninger, K., & Edwards, M. (2008). What the discourse tells us: Talk and indicators of high-level comprehension. *International Journal of Educational Research, 47*, 372–391.

Sweeney, S. (2011). Writing for the instant messaging and text messaging generation: Using new literacies to support writing instruction. *Journal of Adolescent & Adult Literacy, 54*(2), 121–130.

Tompkins, G. (2011). *Teaching writing: Balancing process and product* (6th ed.). Upper Saddle River, NJ: Prentice Hall.

Tucker, M. S. (2011). Standing on the shoulders of giants: An American agenda for education reform. Retrieved from http://www.google.com/search?q=National%20center%20for%20education%20and%20the%20economy&ie=utf-8&oe=utf-8&aq=t&rls=org.mozilla:en-US:official&client=firefox-a&source=hp&channel=np

VanFossen, P. J. (2005). 'Reading and math take so much of the time. . .': An overview of social studies instruction in elementary classrooms in Indiana. *Theory and Research in Social Education, 33*(3), 376–403.

VanSledright, B. (2002). *In search of America's past: Learning to read history in elementary school.* New York, NY: Teachers College Press.

Vasinda, S., & McLeod, J. (2011), Extending Readers Theatre: A powerful and purposeful match with podcasting. *The Reading Teacher, 64*, 486–497.

Vygotksy, L. (1978). *Mind and society: The development of higher psychological processes.* Cambridge, MA: Harvard University Press.

Walmsley, S. (1994). *Children exploring their world: Theme teaching in elementary school.* Portsmouth, NH: Heinemann.

Weiss-Magasic, C. (2012). Writing and science literacy. *The Science Teacher, 79*(1), 41–43.

Wells, G. (1993). *Changing schools from within: Creating communities of inquiry.* Portsmouth, NH: Heinemann.

Wells, G. (2009). *The meaning makers: Learning to talk and talking to learn* (2nd ed.). Bristol, UK: Multilingual Matters.

Wiest, L. (2003, May). Comprehension of mathematical text. *Philosophy of Mathematics Education, 17.* Retrieved from http://people.exeter.ac.uk/PErnest/pome17/lwiest.htm

Wiest, L. R., Higgins, H. J., & Frost, J. H. (2007). Quantitative literacy for social justice. *Equity and Excellence in Education 40*(1), 47–55.

Wills, J. S. (2007). Putting the squeeze on social studies: Managing teaching dilemma in subject areas excluded from state testing. *Teachers College Record, 109*(8), 1980–2046.

Winch, G., Johnston, R., March, P., Ljungdahl, L., & Holliday, M. (2011). *Literacy: Reading, writing, and children's literature* (4th ed.). Sydney, Australia: Oxford University Press.

Wineburg, S. (2001). *Historical thinking and other unnatural acts: Charting the future of teaching the past.* Philadelphia, PA: Temple University Press.

Wineburg, S. (2011). *Reading like a historian: Teaching literacy in middle and high school classrooms.* New York, NY: Teachers College Press.

Wollman-Bonilla, J. E. (2000). Teaching science writing to first graders: Genre learning and recontextualization. *Research in the Teaching of English, 30*, 35–65.

Wood Ray, K. (1999). *Wondrous words: Writers and writing in the elementary classroom.* Urbana, IL: National Council of Teachers of English.

Yopp, R. H., & Yopp, H. K. (2012). Young children's limited and narrow exposure to informational text. *The Reading Teacher, 65*(7), 480–490.

Zhang, S., Duke, N. K., & Jimenez, L. M. (2011). The WWWDOT approach to improving students' critical evaluation of websites. *The Reading Teacher, 65*(2), 150–158.

Index

About the Authors

Cynthia H. Brock is a lecturer in literacy studies at the University of South Australia. Her primary teaching interests include literacy instruction for children in the middle and upper elementary grades, literacy and diversity, and qualitative methods. She studies the literacy learning of upper elementary children from diverse cultural and linguistic backgrounds. She also explores how to work with preservice and inservice teachers to foster the literacy learning of children from diverse backgrounds at the upper elementary level.

Virginia J. Goatley is a faculty member and department chair in the Department of Reading at the University at Albany–SUNY. Her scholarship targets how to bridge literacy research, policy, and practice to improve classroom practice. Her recent federally funded grants focus on the literacy coursework in teacher preparation programs and the implementation of a clinically rich teacher preparation program.

Taffy E. Raphael is a professor of literacy education at the University of Illinois at Chicago. Her research interests include comprehension and writing instruction, frameworks for literacy curriculum and instruction, and whole-school reform. She received the International Reading Association's Outstanding Teacher Educator in Reading Award in 1997 and the Literacy Research Association's Oscar Causey Award for Lifetime Contributions to Literacy Research in 2008. Raphael served on the board of directors of the International Reading Association and the board of the Literacy Research Association, where she also served as treasurer and president. Raphael teaches courses in literacy pedagogy, theory and research, and seminars in literacy research design and literacy leadership.

Elisabeth Trost-Shahata taught 4th-grade English language learners (ELLs) in the Chicago Public Schools for 12 years and is now a bilingual/ESL specialist for the district. She is also an adjunct lecturer at the University of Illinois at Chicago. Her primary teaching interests lie in inspiring a love of reading and writing in students of all ages for whom

English is a new language, especially refugee and newcomer ELLs. She also enjoys supporting preservice and inservice teachers as they improve their teaching of ELLs. She is a passionate advocate for bilingualism and biliteracy in our global age.

Catherine M. Weber is an assistant professor in the Mary Lou Fulton Teachers College at Arizona State University. She is a former elementary teacher and literacy coach who has spent the majority of her career working with diverse learners in high-poverty urban settings. Her research interests include professional development and sustainable school reform. Her passion is helping teachers raise instructional rigor and create curricular coherence to ensure high levels of learning and equal opportunities for all students.